KNOW WE
ARE HERE

KNOW WE ARE HERE

VOICES OF NATIVE CALIFORNIA RESISTANCE

EDITED WITH AN INTRODUCTION
BY TERRIA SMITH

Heyday, Berkeley, California

Library of Congress Cataloging-in-Publication Data

Names: Smith, Terria, editor.
Title: Know we are here : voices of native California resistance / edited with an
    introduction by Terria Smith.
Description: Berkeley, California : Heyday, [2023] | Includes bibliographical references.
Identifiers: LCCN 2022052192 (print) | LCCN 2022052193 (ebook) | ISBN
    9781597146067 (paperback) | ISBN 9781597146074 (epub)
Subjects: LCSH: Indian activists—California. | Indians of North America—Colonization—
    California. | LCGFT: Essays.
Classification: LCC E78.C15 K585 2023 (print) | LCC E78.C15 (ebook) | DDC
    979.4004/97—dc23/eng/20221108
LC record available at https://lccn.loc.gov/2022052192
LC ebook record available at https://lccn.loc.gov/2022052193

Cover photograph of Weshoyot Alvitre (Tongva/Scottish): "Weshoyot" 2021 © by Cara Romero (Chemehuevi)
Cover Design: Tima Lotah Link (Šmuwič Chumash)
Interior Design and Typesetting: Tima Lotah Link (Šmuwič Chumash)

This book was published with the generous support of the Humboldt Area Foundation's Native Cultures Fund.

Published by Heyday
P.O. Box 9145, Berkeley, California 94709
(510) 549-3564
heydaybooks.com

Printed in East Peoria, Illinois, by Versa Press, Inc.

10 9 8 7 6 5 4 3 2 1

IN HONOR OF
THOSE WHO
RESISTED
SO THAT
WE COULD LIVE.

CONTENTS

TERRIA SMITH

I had a friend in college who was consistently pointing out that the root word of *ignorance* is *ignore*. Thus, she believed that someone was making the choice to ignore something. I agree. This is something I see all the time in the work that I do. People claim their ignorance is unintentional when actually it is a thin excuse to ignore the existence of tribal people in California. It's certainly a conscious act. I am convinced of that. Tribes in this state have a lot of physical visibility.

Everywhere.

If you drive across the state, on almost all of our major highways you'll see clearly visible signs that mark where tribal reservations are. In the north there are signs for Table Bluff Reservation, Big Lagoon Rancheria, the Yurok Tribe, and many others along 101. In the south, along I-10 from Los Angeles to Phoenix, you will find the Morongo Band of Mission Indians, Agua Caliente Band of Cahuilla Indians, Cabazon Band of Mission Indians, and the Twenty-Nine Palms Band of Mission Indians. The I-8 is officially named the Kumeyaay Highway and goes through Campo Kumeyaay Nation, the Viejas Band of the Kumeyaay Nation, and Fort Yuma Quechan Tribe in Winterhaven. Also along Highway 101, you have signs for Pinoleville, Coyote Valley, Round Valley, and Robinson Rancheria.

There are cities, towns, and parks all up and down the state with names derived from California tribal languages, including (but certainly not limited to): *Aguanga*, *Azusa*, *Cahuenga*, *Petaluma*, Point *Mugu*, *Ojai*, Rancho *Cucamonga*, *Sisquoc*, *Tehachapi*, *Yucaipa*, and *Yosemite*.

In the city of Palm Springs (half of which is the Agua Caliente reservation), you have several streets named after Cahuilla families: *Andreas*, *Arenas*, *Belardo*, and Vista *Chino*.

I could go on with contemporary geography alone to make this case for physical visibility. But the bottom line is this: when there are well over one hundred federal tribal reservations, and when there are also more than fifty tribes that are unrecognized (many in some of the state's largest urban areas), there is going to be a presence absolutely everywhere. No matter where you turn, there is no denying that there are tribal nations all over California.

Yet still there are people—both those who are not Native American as well as people who were relocated from tribes in other parts of the country—who react in surprise when I introduce myself as Desert Cahuilla, a Native person from a tribe in California indigenous to the Coachella Valley, where there are five reservations. There are people who act like they don't know we are here. And a lot of these folks should know better because it's their job to.

Before I came to be the Heyday Berkeley Roundhouse director, I used to work in television. Specifically, I worked for an Indigenous-focused television network in Southern California. (That's how a lot of tribal folks still remember and identify me.) One time, I went out to a powwow and I interviewed a young Kumeyaay man who was an alum of San Diego State University. He talked about how while he was a student, instead of spending all his time learning, he had to teach his own history professors about local tribes. I find this particularly unacceptable because San Diego County is home to more reservations than any other county in the United States.

California itself is home to more tribes than any other state in the country, with more than six hundred thousand Native Americans living here (according to the 2020 US Census).

The persistence of this ignorance has many adverse ramifications. I remember when the 2016 movement was going on in Standing Rock, North Dakota, against the construction of the Dakota Access Oil Pipeline. Though the movement had support from Native people here in California, there were also a number of people who said things like "Where was all of this attention when we were trying to get the dams off of the Klamath River?" and "Where was everybody when we were trying to protect our sacred sites when the 101 bypass was being built?" And I wondered why there wasn't this type of attention when I reported on the water being polluted on my reservation in Torres Martinez. (It has been about eight years since I produced a story about this environmental harm, and the water remains polluted to this day.)

Some issues—including land reclamation in the redwoods, protection of burial sites, and indigenous language revitalization—have received attention in international news media, including publications and websites like *Al Jazeera*, the *Guardian*, the *Los Angeles Times*, the *New York Times*, and the *Washington Post*.

These issues should be at the forefront of the California collective consciousness. They impact everyone. But for some reason, most of the time if the public knows anything it's usually related to tribal gaming. And rightly so. Tribal gaming has been responsible for the economic growth and prosperity of many California regions. I remember as a young person how Palm Springs was basically turning into a ghost town before the Spa Casino opened. People used to call Temecula a "cow town," and now folks are practically falling over each other to try to raise their families there.

I personally associate the places I go to in California with the tribes that are from there. There is nowhere you can go in the state where there is not a reservation, rancheria, or tribal headquarters nearby. To be fair, California is filled with people with lineages from all over the world, and even culturally attentive people overlook tribes in the midst of the country's most populous state. But for those who still say they are unfamiliar with these lands and their people, there are resources—such as the Native Land app—that anyone with an smartphone can access. Knowledge is accessible, and ignorance is no longer an excuse.

Anyone who has been to Arizona, New Mexico, Oklahoma, Washington, or Alaska has experienced the region's tribal cultures all around them. This is something that is embraced and part of the identity of those states. A lot of people travel to these places specifically to interact with tribal communities and cultures. I am one of those people. As a Native person, I really appreciate going to places like Arizona—which is only a couple of hours from my reservation—and seeing tribal people nearly everywhere: at the gas station, in the grocery store. Some of these folks are even my friends. It's an incredible feeling to be a part of a visible population.

There is one region in California I have been to that is similar: the northwest. In places like Humboldt County, III facial tattoos are common, women wear basket hats, and parents carry their babies in baskets to the mall. This is where I went for my undergraduate education. When I was there I admired the young Native women I went to school with. While a lot of students were coming to class in their pajamas and sweatpants as though they had just rolled out of bed, across campus these young ladies wore their beautiful long hair tied in elk bone and adorned themselves with regal abalone necklaces. The beauty of the culture itself was resistance.

In my line of work I have learned that resistance takes many different forms. It does not always look like activism, but it can and sometimes does. At times we have to go into the streets to take a stand against injustice, protect our environment, and defend sacred sites. Language teachers fight the pervasive narrative of impending doom projected onto us, a false claim that our tribal tongues are "dying." Tribal historians look into archives in search of our true stories. Some of us even venture outside of our homelands to find solidarity and commonality with other oppressed peoples.

This book takes a look at all of these types of resistance. The California Native people who have authored these essays and who have been featured in these interviews are themselves activists, attorneys, cultural teachers, historians, scholars, students, tribal leaders, and university professors who have thorough understandings of where they come from. The writings were previously featured in past issues of *News from Native California* magazine or come from books published by Heyday over the past twenty-five years.

The title of this book, *Know We Are Here*, is derived from one of Esselen/Chumash author Deborah Miranda's essays featured here. The cover image of Tongva artist Weshoyot Alvitre was taken by Chemehuevi photographer Cara Romero. It was part of a billboard campaign to make visible the first peoples of Los Angeles.

Ac'ama to everyone who has contributed. I am so proud that this book will join several others in this era when so many other books have been written in recent years *by* California Native peoples, rather than by outsiders who have written *about* California Native peoples. University students in California can now quite possibly have their entire Native American studies curriculum presented to them with books that are all written by California Native authors. In that same respect, my hope is that others will come across this book and learn about California's first people from some of our best and brightest.

HISTORIES OF
RESISTANCE

"DEAR SONORA": WRITING TO A FOURTH GRADER ABOUT HER PROJECT

DEBORAH A. MIRANDA

In 2012, the Ohlone Costanoan Esselen Nation received a request from a sharp fourth grader asking about the Native experience in California missions. Here is that letter, and our response.

Dear Ms. Ramirez,
I am a fourth grader and I am doing my report on Mission Nuestra Senora Dolorosisima de la Soledad. I discovered that Coastanoan and Essellen are some of the names of the tribes that went to the Soledad mission, and I was searching for some info on them when I stumbled across your email address on www.ohlonecostanoanesselennation.org. Me and my mom decided that maybe you could help us/me. Anyway, what I was searching for was the opinion of the Coastanoan and Esselen Native Americans. I want to know if the Native Americans liked the mission, which priests were their favorites . . . stuff like that, and I'm hoping you can help me. If you can help me, or even if you can't, thanks a ton!
Sincerely, Sonora

Dear Sonora (what a great name!),

My sister Louise passed your message on to me; she's very busy as Chair, and since I read about and study California missions in my job, she thought I might be able to help you out. I can tell you right away that writing to California tribes on your own is a smart move—many people don't think to ask us, or they think we are all dead. Still here!

You wanted to know the Ohlone-Esselen-Costanoan opinion of the missions. That's a tough question. Some Indian people will tell you that the missions were great, and brought us Catholicism and agriculture; others will tell you that anything that kills about 80 percent of your people can't be good.

California Indians were actually doing fine before the Spanish, Mexicans, and Americans arrived. Our ancestors had everything they needed, including Indian religions, leaders, music, languages, jobs, and education. But because our ancestors' traditions were different from the way Europeans did those things, lots of Spanish people thought Indians needed "civilizing." Of course, Indians were curious about the Spanish, and about their religion, and often helped the Spaniards find food and water, or exchanged things in trade with them, but that did not mean our ancestors wanted to become Spanish. People should be allowed to decide for themselves how they want to live.

Instead, the missionaries made that decision for our ancestors. Sometimes the Spanish priests would "baptize" women and children who came to visit, and then refuse to let them go. The husbands and fathers would come to get them, and were told that they could not see their families unless they, too, allowed themselves to be baptized. Of course, none of the Indians knew what baptism really meant, and when the priests then told them that, once baptized, they could not leave the mission, it was a big surprise. Remember, missionaries and soldiers thought of themselves as "civilized," so they figured

THEY must be right and the Indians wrong. Civilized people don't hurt other people for being different, though. Many Indians today do not think the Spanish were very civilized.

The missionaries did a lot of things that hurt Indian people and families. For example, all little girls over the age of seven had to go sleep in the *monjerio*, a small building with no bathroom and small windows way up taller than anyone could reach. These rooms were dark, smelly, and dirty, and the young women and girls kept in there got sick from germs and lack of fresh air. They were also very homesick for their families. They didn't see their parents much, since during the day the parents were forced to work for the missionaries, doing all the work to build, maintain, and farm for the mission. Our ancestors were also forced to attend the Catholic church, learn prayers in a new language, and take new names in Spanish. None of the Indian ways of living—religions, leaders, music, languages, jobs, and education—were allowed by the Spaniards.

Also, I'm sorry to say, Indians at the mission were whipped with a very heavy, painful leather whip if they broke any of the priests' rules—and since Indians didn't know Spanish, and missionaries didn't know Indian languages, there were a lot of misunderstandings about what the rules were. Plus, of course, sometimes the Indians (who had taken very good care of themselves for thousands of years) didn't think Spanish rules made sense in the first place, so they would do things that were against the rules like gather wild food, go hunting, leave the mission to visit their families elsewhere, marry whom they wanted to marry, or other things they considered part of their rights as human beings. Spaniards punished Indians for doing these simple things with whippings or time in the stocks.

Over time, the European livestock and plants that the Spanish had brought with them to California took over the land, and many basic foods that Indians depended on were destroyed, so our ancestors became very dependent on the European foods from the missions.

Our bodies sometimes could not handle this change in diet, which made it harder for us to get over small illnesses like colds and flu, and big illnesses like European smallpox, measles, and tuberculosis. So many Indians died in the missions that the padres had to keep sending Spanish soldiers out to capture more Indians to do the work of running cattle, farming, building, weaving, cooking, and doing all the chores a big mission requires.

You might be wondering, why would the Indians put up with all this? I suggest you look up things like "California mission rebellion" or "California mission revolt" on the internet (a better phrase would be "California Mission Wars," but you probably won't find anything using that search term—can you guess why?).

I think everyone, historians and Indians alike, agrees that missionization was a disaster for the Indians: our estimated population numbers went from about one million to fifteen thousand in just under two hundred years. We lost almost all of our land, all of our natural resources (which provided food and shelter); many of us lost our language, religion, and communities. Can you imagine if eight out of every ten people you know died when another group of people showed up and took over your town?

So mostly, the missions were not that much fun for Indians. An Indian baby born in a California mission lived only to be seven or eight years old; some disease or other would kill them before they could grow up. Also, because of a European strain of a disease called syphilis, many Indian men and women could no longer have babies, so there were no new kids to replace the people who died. Every time an old person died, it was like an entire library of knowledge, history, and stories burned down. That's tough to survive!

There were many bad consequences from the California missions for California Indians. Those bad consequences continued on through the Mexican era and into the American era. The hardest consequence was losing our homelands. The Spaniards made us move into the missions, but sixty-five years later when the missions closed down, all of our land had been taken by other non-Indian people. We had nowhere to go, no way to feed ourselves, no food, shelter, or clothing. Mexicans, who governed California after the Spanish, used Indians as free labor on their large ranches. For a meal and a place to sleep, Indians worked almost like slaves for the Mexicans, just to stay alive. Most mission Indian communities were broken up, and it was even harder for tribal members to stay connected than in the missions.

But as bad as that was, after the Mexican government came the American government, with laws that were even worse—American law prevented Indians from owning land, voting, or taking a white person to court for even the worst crimes against Indians. The US Congress passed a law giving millions of dollars to Americans to round up and kill Indians who were "in the way." In my family, we have stories about ancestors who answered a knock at the door, opened the door, and were shot for the bounty money! As late as 1866, Indians could be bought and sold just like slaves in the American South—and thousands were, especially women and children. Even Indians like my great-great-great-great-great grandfather, Fructuoso Cholom Real, who received land in a Mexican land grant after the missions were closed down, ended up losing their land to Americans.

But some of us did survive, and in California our communities are slowly growing and working to recover from those bad consequences. It's hard when many of us, like the Esselen, don't have any land (no reservation, no place to meet). Whenever we have our annual gathering, for example, we have to pay someone to use their land. So we don't have too many gatherings. This is one of the many consequences of the missions that continue into our lives today. Like several other California tribes, the Esselen are petitioning the US government for recognition—that means we would be eligible to get back a small piece of government "surplus" land in our homeland that we could use as a center, apply for educational scholarships that are only available to federally recognized tribes, and receive some basic health benefits.

It's funny, but even though I can prove that my family history was Indian all the way back to 1770, when the Spaniards started keeping paper records, the government still considers me "non-Indian"!

I hope you research hard and learn a lot about the missions and the California Indians who had to live there. It was a crazy time, a hard time, and a sad time. It's a miracle anyone survived at all. California Indians want our ancestors to be proud of us. We know we are here only because a few of them managed to survive, and used up all of their strength so we could live.

Oh—I realize that I didn't actually answer your question about favorite priests. The Spanish priests, and later the Mexican priests, were human beings with the same gifts and flaws as anyone else. So, like most people, some priests were considered "kind" and others were considered "mean." Father Serra, for instance, wrote in his letters about how much he loved the Indians, and how badly he felt when the Spanish soldiers hurt or killed Indians. But as kind as he seemed, Father Serra never questioned whether the missions should be built or maintained. He never thought to ask, as you did, Sonora, what Indians thought of the missions or the priests. He believed that the Spaniard's way of living was the ONLY way of living. So in his view, Indians who lived differently had to be made to change—even if it meant killing them, or spreading disease, or denying them human rights.

This way of thinking is called "colonization." Colonization, or in California what we call "missionization," is a cruel and unkind way to treat other people. It means, basically, that a colonizer doesn't think Indians or Native people are really human beings. It is a very strange, selfish way of seeing the world.

Good luck with your report,

Deborah A. Miranda

FIDEL'S PLACE

GREG SARRIS

Three days after the Indian—I'll call him Fidel—avenged
the assault on his wife and slayed the young rancher who'd
committed the horrible deed, the posse of vigilantes pursuing him
found him, not near the small settlement of Marshall but across
Tomales Bay on a ridge, and not in a thicket of coyote brush and
low-growing fir, where he might've hidden, but in the middle of an
open grassland. Seemingly oblivious to the sound of approaching
horses, he was standing, taking in the view, continuing to look over
his shoulder at the expansive Pacific and then back across the bay to
the eastern hills from which he'd come. Even when the men shouted
threats, dismounted, and aimed their bayonet-clad rifles at him, he
did not waver. He didn't look as if he'd been running for days; his
clothes on that fogless morning were clean, and he wore a brightly
colored shirt, perhaps white or scarlet, creating the impression, along
with his indifference to their approach, that he actually wanted to
be found. Surrender.

The men continued to bark orders, bayonets jutting from their
rifles only feet from him, and all he did was drop his gaze to the

grass where he'd been standing, then look back to the open prairie, his head twisted around, even as they marched him, shackled, down to the boat that would carry him across the water to Marshall.

———

I was twelve or thereabouts when I first heard about Fidel. A friend's mother, I believe a descendant of Fidel, told the story. Like many Coast Miwok from Tomales Bay, my friend's mother had moved north to Santa Rosa a couple decades before, shortly after World War II, looking for work, and she often reminisced with her sisters about "the old days in Marshall"—sharing stories not just with each other but for any kids who sat at her kitchen table and listened.

I never liked the story. I found it moralizing, admonishing— for while this man Fidel had great powers, including the ability to shape-shift into a hummingbird, which would have allowed him to escape his captors, he could not use them because he had broken the tacitly understood rule that those who possessed these powers should not commit murder. But after decades of dislocation and abuse (this story took place in the late 1860s or early 1870s), to find your wife gagged and tied under the thrall of a white man and not do anything—or to get punished for seeking justice—just didn't seem fair. Hearing the tale, I, probably like others listening in, sublimated the part of the story I didn't like and focused instead on Fidel's revenge, how he survived. "If you go to Marshall on a night when there is no fog," my friend's mother said, "you can sometimes see on that treeless ridge across the water an enormous green light."

———

For Coast Miwok people, like all Indigenous peoples of central California, the landscape was nothing less than a richly layered text, a sacred book; each ocean cove, even the smallest seemingly unassuming rock or tract of open grassland—each feature of the natural world was a mnemonic peg on which individuals could see

16

a story connected to other stories and thus know and find themselves home. Villages, indeed entire nations, were not only associated with particular locales but actually named after them. Hence, the tribal nation that occupied most of the territory encompassing what is now called Point Reyes National Seashore called itself Olema, Coyote's Home. A large village overlooking Drakes Bay was Pusuluma, Olivella Shell Ridge; and the open grassland ridge and shoreline just north of Lairds Landing on Tomales Bay, where vigilantes found Fidel on that fogless summer morning, was called Calupetamal, Hummingbird Coast.

By the late 1860s or early 1870s, the landscape of the region had been greatly transformed, much of the homescape trampled, unreadable. The fir forests were logged, the waterways dammed or dredged, the herds of elk and pronghorn all but gone. Overgrazing and foreign seed in the dung of the cattle and horses combined to unsettle the prairie grasslands, replacing the deep-rooted perennial bunchgrasses and sedges with exotic annuals like European oatgrass. European settlement thus spelled dis-settlement; and for the Natives the dis-settlement was both personal and historical, psychological and environmental.

Members of the Olema nation, and of Guaulen, just south of the Olema, were among the first Coast Miwok to be taken into the missions, specifically into Mission Dolores in San Francisco, as early as 1818. Many survivors of the missions and the subsequent Mexican rancho period ended up on a tract of land near present-day Nicasio. When these survivors were booted out of Nicasio by Americans in the early 1860s, many went west to Tomales Bay and settled along the shore. Today, however, no known Coast Miwok trace their ancestry back to an Olema village; most of the mission survivors originated from eastern locales, and many were the descendants of intermarriage between Spanish or Mexican settlers. Yet stories of the place persisted; perhaps some Olema survivors had returned to—or even led others to—the region. In the old tradition, the survivors rooted themselves to the place and began to call themselves Tomales Bay Indians.

———

I saw the green light. On one of those many trips from Santa Rosa to Marshall in the middle of the night, a dozen of us packed into a car or onto a truck bed, didn't I see the ball of green light atop the ridge across the water? "I see it," someone always said. Maybe I didn't see it and only know it in my imagination. The shape of the grassland ridge that rises above the bay was there, visible even in the dark night.

And it is there today, the open prairie of Tomales Point, bordered by brush and sparse live oak, not unlike the prairie grasslands elsewhere along the seashore. I've made several trips to this place in recent years, stood in the grass and taken in the views. Tule elk have been reintroduced, but where they once roamed freely, now they are contained by fences maintained for the local dairy ranchers: more black-and-white Holsteins dot the peninsula's grassland than elk. Yet always the man Fidel rises up from the grass, visible before me, bright shirt, his demeanor resolved, and I am set to wonder about him, though now it's not the green light or the drama of his last days that intrigues me but the question regarding this place—why he stopped in the open, as if his only reason for fleeing the law was to come to this particular spot.

The grasslands were always a safe haven, not only for herds of elk and pronghorn to graze, and for us to hunt, but also as refuge from the grizzlies less visible in the forests, behind brush. Villages were always located adjacent to grasslands, and in fact, controlled burning of the grasslands kept the brush and encroaching trees in check. After European settlement, when Natives were forbidden to burn, much of the grassland was taken over by coyote brush and Douglas fir.

Fidel, though, wasn't hiding. What safety, then, in the open space? He could've run south from Marshall, not turned northward below the bay, and run out onto the narrowing peninsula between ocean and bay, where he would be trapped eventually. Did he simply want to go where he had views? Was there something in the place concerning his totem hummingbird that he had to reconcile before his death? Or was it a memory, certainly of his wife, the strength and delicacy of her fingers as she held a basket and a seed beater while collecting seed for pinole, and, as she went along there, how the hem of her dress caught and lifted atop the grass stalk?

Then Fidel is laughing at me. For, once again, frustrated by my pondering, I follow him across the water to the hanging noose, to the scaffold on which he stands, the mob below, jeering American settlers, somber Indians in the distance, and at last I understand something. It is the grassland itself, the safety it gives in memory. There is the space, yes, on which memory paints its lore. But it is in the grass too—perennials, annuals, roots—grasses that reveal the shape of the land from time immemorial, and continue to rise up there again and again. The prairie, so empty, so full. Is that what Fidel sought—that understanding in the grass?

He is gone, the scaffold empty; and there on that grassland ridge, a light in the brain, he stands, laughing. "What more?" he says. "You told the story."

HUTNYILSHS: THE BLACK DOG NATION

MICHAEL CONNOLLY MISKWISH

I n the time of the *sh'mulls* (clans), before the invasion by the Spaniards, the *sh'mull* leaders of the Kumeyaay people were called *kwaipai*. They were valued for their wisdom and judgement, often acting as arbitrators and counselors. But when strong leadership was needed, such as times of disaster and war, a *kachut* would be chosen to lead.

One of the most powerful *kachuts* of the 1800s was Hutnyilsh, or Black Dog. At his greatest power, Hutnyilsh had over one thousand warriors from many *sh'mulls* under his command.

Hutnyilsh was the third generation of *kachuts* to lead what became known to the Spaniards and Mexicans as the Hutnyilshs. (I use "Spaniard" to refer to people serving the Spanish Empire, although ethnically, Indians and mixed-blood Indians made up the majority of most of the expeditions, with priests and officers more

---

Bibliographic references for this essay can be found in the References and Notes section at the back of the book.

likely to be European.) Hutnyilsh's grandfather, the first Hutnyilsh (Hutnyilsh [I]), is part of the story of the first entry of Dominican priests into the southern lands of the Kumeyaay and the formation of the "Hutnyilsh Nation." The story of the Hutnyilshs is complex and covers more than fifty-three years. Originally friends and protectors of the Spanish missions, the Hutnyilshs became active military allies of the Mexicans, even fighting against other Indian peoples. Ultimately, they turned against the missions, leaving them to their abandonment and destruction.

To tell this story, we must go back in time to the first invasions of what would be called California.

The first attempts to colonize California were made by Hernán Cortés in 1532 and 1535. Due to his failures and the reports of other expeditions (Cabrillo, Ulloa, Vizcaíno) regarding the fierceness of Indian nations, California was long considered an unconquerable territory.

On the mainland, the Spaniards had suffered major setbacks as they attempted to expand their reach beyond the large city-states of central Mexico. Their system of co-opting the Aztec tribute system by empowering the local Indian nobles did not work when they encountered more decentralized nations. The Spanish, alongside their Aztec and Tlaxcalan allies, won at considerable cost the Mixtón War of 1540–1542 against the Caxcan Nation. This was followed by the Chichimeca War of 1550–1590 against the Chichimeca Confederation (composed mainly of the Guachichil, Pame, Guamare, and Zacateco nations), which resulted in defeat for the Spanish military strategy (Schmal 2003; Powell 1952; Santa Maria 2003). It was apparent to the Spaniards that the costs of maintaining multiple forts in the Chichimeca region and providing security on the supply routes were not sustainable. In 1584 the Bishop of Guadalajara proposed a "Christian remedy" to the war, substituting missions to win over the populations instead of the "fire and blood" policy of the military.

By 1586 Viceroy Álvaro Manrique de Zúñiga had begun removing soldiers from the forts and replacing them with Christianized Indians to use as examples. In 1590 a policy called "purchase for peace" was implemented, where large quantities of tools, food, and clothing were supplied to the Chichimeca. The development of this "Christian remedy" for the Chichimeca would, over the coming decades, be refined into the colonial mission strategy that would be used in California; in contemporary parlance this could be referred to as the weaponization of the missions.

After the establishment of the Manila galleon trade route in 1565 (partially the result of Cabrillo's expedition of 1542–1543), Spanish ships loaded with wealth regularly sailed along the California coast. The Pacific crossing from the Philippines was long and arduous. The galleon crews were often conscripted and hostile toward the officers and supplies could run dangerously low. This was compounded by the fear of piracy for the lone ships traveling without escort. The galleon *Santa Ana* was looted and burned in 1587 by the English privateer Thomas Cavendish.

The fear of pirates and the need for a more northern port after the Pacific crossing led to Sebastián Vizcaíno's expedition in 1602–1603. Vizcaíno saw Monterey as the ideal port location to meet the Spaniards' needs but could not garner enough support to implement his recommendation. Throughout the seventeenth century, many attempts were made to colonize California. The government tried to use commercial inducements, authorizing contracts for pearl trading with the California Indians in hopes of establishing colonies. Royally funded expeditions were conducted under Carbonel, Córdova, Ortega, Porter y Casanate, Piñadero, and Lucenilla. All of these failed.

In 1679 a royal enterprise was entrusted to Don Isidro Atondo y Antillón. Two short-term settlements in Baja California were established and then abandoned by 1685. Efforts were suspended when the Tarahumaras revolted that year, and it would be twelve years before another effort was made (Kino 1919).

Ultimately, in 1697, the Viceroy of Mexico authorized the Jesuit order of the Catholic Church to establish missions in California. The Jesuit order was the recent beneficiary of the Pious Fund of the Californias, which had been founded that year to sponsor the creation of missions in the region (McDonald 1934). At first unsuccessful, they were able on their second try to establish a mission in Monqui territory in 1697, which they named Loreto. By 1767, they had established fourteen missions in Baja California (Duggan 2016).

In 1767, the Jesuits were ordered to leave the Spanish Empire, including California. The Franciscans took over the missions and continued the Jesuit process of gradually moving up the California peninsula. News of British and Russian movement southward from the north increased the urgency to move into Alta California. Father Junípero Serra introduced a plan to accelerate the process by establishing missions, beginning with one at San Diego and then Monterey. Serra also met with the Dominican Order, which was concerned about being left out of the move into the Jesuit territories of California. At a 1768 meeting, the Franciscans and the Dominicans agreed to split the California territory into a southern component under the Dominicans and a northern component under the Franciscans. Although the wording of the agreement left room for argument on the true location of the dividing line, it was set at the 32.5° latitude, roughly through the middle of the Kumeyaay Nation and close to the present-day US–Mexican border (Meigs 1935).

In 1769, the first overland traversing of Kumeyaay lands was led by Captain Fernando Rivera y Moncada. He was accompanied by Franciscan Fr. Juan Crespí. This was the vanguard of the overland expedition of Governor Gaspar de Portolá and Fr. Junípero Serra. As reported by Father Crespí, the Kumeyaay tracked and harassed the expedition on their route. At village sites, Kumeyaay were generally wary and courteous, as well as curious about the travelers; however, they kept their weapons at the ready. At one point an ambush was set up but the Spaniards detected and avoided it. It was also apparent that the Kumeyaay understood the range of Spanish firearms, keeping just beyond the effective range of the weapons.

By the time of Portolá and Serra's second expedition, the Kumeyaay's communication networks informed them of the ships that had anchored at San Diego and the establishment of a base of operations there. The Kumeyaay probably considered it prudent to accommodate the Spaniards until a full assessment could be made of the Spanish agenda. Portolá and Serra found the Kumeyaay much more accommodating and friendly and they experienced little conflict traversing the lands. In his journals, Serra interpreted the friendliness as a sign of eagerness to become Christians. It was noted that there were smoke signals on the mountains to their east and Serra reported that many Cochimí neophytes abandoned the expedition as they neared the territory of the Kumeyaay (Beebe and Senkewicz 2013).

While the Franciscans under Serra began to create their network of missions in Alta California, the Dominicans were working to expand the existing Baja California mission system. The Dominicans had founded missions up to the boundary of the Kumeyaay Nation at San Vicente by 1780. After the destruction of the mission at San Diego in 1775 and the destruction of two missions on the Colorado River in 1781 by the Quechan, the Dominicans were reluctant to move into the Kumeyaay lands. With the loss of an overland route from the Colorado River and the difficulties of resupply by sea, the need for a more secure overland route up the peninsula was critical. In 1783, the governor of the peninsula, under order from the king of Spain, intervened and ordered the Dominicans to move into the Kumeyaay lands or risk losing their authority.

By this time, the Kumeyaay were well aware of the entrenched presence of Spaniards in San Diego and were now hostile to this invasion into their lands. The Mission San Vicente had to build a presidio to defend against repeated Indian attacks. Finally, in 1787, the Dominicans made their first attempt to enter Kumeyaay lands but were forced to retreat from the Kumeyaay forces. The Spaniards returned with a larger force and were able to capture a Kumeyaay leader in battle. The Spaniards were able to communicate a desire for peace and trade. They then released the leader, who met with his people and returned with an agreement to the establishment of a Spanish presence at what would become Mission San Miguel, north of present-day Ensenada.

This first entry by the Dominicans into Kumeyaay lands was done with much trepidation. They were under instruction to avoid antagonizing any of the surrounding Kumeyaay. Governor Pedro Fages described the local Kumeyaay as the most *bronco* (wild or unbroken) of the Indians (Meigs 1935). This flexibility in strategy was no doubt an important factor in the relationship that developed over the next decades.

One of the leaders who rose to prominence during this time was a man named Hutnyilsh [I]. In those early days of the Mission San Miguel, Hutnyilsh [I] made an alliance with the Spaniards, where he agreed to protect the mission in return for autonomy from the colonial mission system. His legacy was handed down to his son and grandson, who both took the same name.

The destruction of the missions on the Colorado River by the Quechan had cut off the overland route from mainland New Spain into California. The Spaniards tried to re-open the route by establishing the Mission Santa Catalina near the Kumeyaay in Paipai territory. From there they engaged in unsuccessful military operations against the Cocopah and Quechan. Eventually, the Spanish military abandoned the outpost. Christianized Kumeyaay, Paipai, and Kiliwa were left to take care of themselves at the mission, with only occasional visits by priests. The Christianized Indians of Santa

Catalina made peace with their non-Christian neighbors and eventually even supported them in some of their battles against the Spaniards. Ultimately, the non-Christian Kumeyaay and Cocopah destroyed the mission; it was later re-established as the Santa Catarina Mission (Panich 2010).

In 1810, probably during the reign of Hutnyilsh's father, Hutnyilsh [II], there was a general uprising against the Dominicans in Baja, but the peace held with the Hutnyilsh Nation.

During the Mexican War of Independence (1810–1821), money and supplies dried up and the missions had to fend for themselves in many respects. Due to their lack of agricultural success, the missions in Kumeyaay territory had already shifted to ranching and the fur trade (Lacson 2015). This change in economic direction accelerated during the war. Prohibitions against teaching Indians to ride horses were ignored (Panich 2017). In fact, even non-Christian Indians were hired, at times, to assist with the ranch work while trade in seal and otter furs was undertaken with Christian and non-Christian Indians alike. The mission priests were openly defiant of Spanish authorities on the illicit trade in hides, declaring that they could get ten pesos per hide selling to foreigners in contrast to the Spanish price of seven (Barajas and Duggan 2018).

Indians outside the protection of Hutnyilsh were subject to forcible conscription into the labor force and pressured into conversion. Manuel C. Rojo's notes, written from 1857 until they were submitted to the Bancroft Library in 1879, provide many such stories.

———

THE STORY OF JANITÍN

This story probably occurred during the late 1820s or 1830s,
as the Rosarito Rancho was established in 1827.

I and two relatives of mine came down from the Nejí
Mountains to Rosarito Beach to catch clams, to eat and
take back to the mountain as we were accustomed to
doing every year; we did no harm to anyone on the way,
and on the beach we thought only of catching and drying
clams to take to our settlement.

While we were doing this, we saw two men on horses
racing toward where we were; my relatives, of course, were
afraid and began to run away as fast as they could, hiding
in the thick willow grove which existed at that time in
the gully of Rosarito Rancho.

When I saw that I was alone, I became afraid of
those men too, and I ran toward the forest to join my
companions, but it was too late, because just then they
caught me and lassoed me and dragged me a long ways,
banging me around a great deal on the branches over
which they dragged me, pulling me, lassoed as I was, as
fast as their horses would go; after this they tied me up
with my arms behind me and took me on to the mission
of San Miguel, making me go almost full speed to keep
up with the trot of their horses, and when I would stop
a little to catch my breath, they whipped me with straps
that they had with them, making me understand by signs
that I had to move quickly; after going a long ways in
this fashion, they slowed down and whipped me so that
I would always keep pace with their horses.

When we arrived at the mission, they shut me up
in a room for a week; the father would make me go to

28

his room and would talk to me through an interpreter, telling me to become a Christian, and he spoke to me about many things that I didn't understand; and Cuñur (that was the interpreter's name) advised me to do as the father told me, because they weren't going to let me go and it would go very badly for me if I didn't consent to it; they gave me corn *atole* which I didn't like because I wasn't used to that food; but what was I going to do if there was nothing else?

One day they threw water on my head and gave me salt to eat, and with this the interpreter told me that now I was a Christian and that my name was Jesús; I didn't know anything about this, and I endured everything because in the end I was a poor Indian and I had nothing else to do but resign myself and endure everything they might do to me.

On the day following my baptism they took me out to work with the rest of the Indians, and put me to work cleaning up a plot of corn; since I didn't know how to handle the hoe which they gave me, after hoeing for a short while I cut my foot and couldn't continue working with it; instead I began to tear out the weeds with my hand, and thus I didn't finish the job they gave me. In the afternoon they whipped me because I didn't finish my job, and on the following day the same thing happened to me as happened the day before; every day they whipped me unjustly because I didn't do what I didn't know how to do, and thus I was for several days until I found a way to escape; but they followed my trail and caught me in La Zorra; there they lassoed me like the first time and took me to the mission, martyrizing me on the way; when we arrived the father was walking the corridor of the house, and he ordered them to tie me to the pillory and punish me; they gave me so many lashes that I lost consciousness, and I don't know when they untied me from the pillory, nor what happened for many hours afterwards. I was several days without being able to get up from the ground where they laid me out, and I still have the marks from the lashes that they gave me at that time on my back. (Rojo [1879] 1972)

Janitín fled again as soon as he was able and managed to remain free in the mountains until the missions were destroyed years later.

———

By the mid-1820s, the Mexican Republic had been established and sought to bring a new direction to California. The political elite under the Spanish Empire continued to hold power under the new government. Many of the elite wanted to carve up the region into ranchos and take charge of mission lands. Mexico City resisted and this caused a split in the Mexican population. Californians began arming as they separated into factions preparing for war.

The trigger for this was the arrival of the new governor, Lieutenant Colonel Manuel Victoria, who represented the centrist philosophy of Mexico City and halted the secularization of the missions started under his predecessor, José María de Echeandía. Victoria, with a force of thirty men, confronted Echeandía's 150 men under the command of Captain Pablo de la Portilla near Los Angeles in 1831. Victoria was wounded and conceded to the victors. No clear leader emerged as southern Californians under Echeandía maneuvered for power against the northern Californians led by Agustín Zamorano. Echeandía even started recruiting and arming Indians to support the rebellion (Killea 1966).

A new governor arrived in 1833, José Figueroa, who pardoned the participants in the revolt. His efforts at undoing Echeandía's secularization efforts were short-lived, as the Mexico City government passed a sweeping secularization act in August 1833. The Secularization Act was supposed to end the colonial mission system but California was able to get an exemption in 1835, which allowed the system to persist into the 1840s. Even so, secularization supporters, known as liberals, moved quickly to implement their own ideas of secularization. Large areas of land were allocated as ranchos under the plan, triggering a revolt throughout much of the Kumeyaay lands.

Both Christianized and non-Christianized Kumeyaay then united and began a series of attacks on the ranchos. Cocopah and Quechan warriors joined in some of the battles. In the first half of 1834, the Santa Catarina Indians joined with the Cocopah to attack the Mexicans. The Mexicans were warned by Cota Blanco, an Indian from the Mission Santa Catarina. Smoke signals across the mountain range signaled that a general uprising was coming. Many Mexicans and Christian Indians fled to Guadalupe Valley to take advantage of the protection of Hutnyilsh, while others fled to the Mission San Vicente Ferrer. In 1836, Hutnyilsh assisted in defending San Diego against a combined force of Kumeyaay and Quechan led by *kachuts* Martin, Cartucho, and Pedro Pablo. The residents of San Diego were so fearful that they crowded at the end of the Point Loma peninsula, hoping to evacuate by ship.

During this time, Hutnyilsh continued to honor the agreement that had started with his grandfather. The cost was extreme as it pitted his warriors against other Indian warriors in many battles through the 1830s. By 1840, the Hutnyilshs were at their weakest in decades from the fighting.

Father Félix Caballero was actively engaged in the smuggling trade and had accumulated a sizable fortune by 1840 (Rojo [1879] 1972). Needing more manpower for the mission and unable to attract enough volunteers, Caballero now decided to breach the agreement with the Hutnyilshs and began to forcibly convert people of the

Hutnyilsh Nation. After fifty-three years of cooperation and much sacrifice, this betrayal could not go unanswered.

———

Manuel Rojo's notes also include interviews with two participants in the events on Saturday, February 1, 1840, at Mission Guadalupe.

Interview with Maria Gracia,
neophyte of Mission Guadalupe:

Jatiñil [Hutnyilsh] marched on the Mission at Guadalupe. Lieutenant Garraleta and seventeen soldiers had left the Mission to drill several miles away leaving only one corporal at the Mission. The Corporal was hit with a war club and subsequently killed. The Kumeyaay woman Maria Gracia, a neophyte at Guadalupe, later recounted her story.

"I was setting the table at which the Father was going to eat and I looked out the dining room window which opened on the patio and saw everything all full of blood and Corporal Orantes dead; I saw that the Hutnyilshs were killing Francisco and José Antonio, neophyte Indians of Mission San Miguel who had come to Guadalupe to plant wheat and barley on the table lands of El Tigre; the Hutnyilshs took their time doing this while the Father and I, seeing what was happening, became filled with fear and went to take refuge in the church; but considering that the gentiles would not respect the main altar where we thought of taking shelter first, we went up to the choir because there we were less obvious to those who entered the church; the Father, when he saw that they were shouting at him to kill him and that all their rage was directed towards him, begged me for God's sake not to give him away, promising me that if the Virgin Mary got him out of that conflict he was in, he would give me everything I might need from then on in order to live leisurely and with no need to serve anyone as long as God remembered me; that's what he told me and he had me sit down on top of him, hiding him with my clothes even from those who might see me; I, frighted [*sic*] to death as I was and without being at all sure about my own life, felt sorry for Father Félix and did everything that he ordered me to do, knowing that if the Indians came to discover that I was hiding him, then they would inevitably kill me, even though they had no intention of harming me, because that's how they are; they never forgive anyone who hides an enemy or a person upon whom they want to take vengeance for something that that person has done to them. I remember all this as though it had just happened right now; I was sitting on top of Father Caballero, having hidden him well with my tunic, when I heard footsteps going up the choir stairs where I was in that position; I felt cold as Hutnyilsh approached with this bow in one hand and said to me; 'How's it going, relative?'; I don't even know that I answered, and I began to cry, begging him not to harm me. 'Don't be afraid,' he told me, 'I haven't ordered anyone killed, but the people who have come with me killed Corporal Orantes and also Francisco and José Antonio; the one I'm looking for is the Father, because he's forcing baptisms on the people of my tribe in order to enslave them in the mission just like you are without enjoying your liberty and living like horses. Where is the Father?' 'Why do you ask me,' I answered, 'when I don't even know how I got here because I'm so afraid from seeing you so mad?' 'Well, I'm going,' he said, and went down without saying another word; in a very short time everything was quiet and, recovering my courage, I went down to the patio; all the Indians had left already, and I could only make out the dust that they raised along the north gulch opposite the mission as they moved toward the mountain." (Rojo [1879] 1972)

It also appears that the attack was coordinated with the Mexican Army. Lieutenant Garraleta had gone to drill his men much further from the mission than normal. Also, Don Juan Machado—son of José Manuel Machado, who was granted the Rancho El Rosario (sometimes translated as Rancho Rosarito) in 1827—reported that he saw Hutnyilsh stop by and converse with Garraleta, shaking his hand and then continuing on to the Mission Guadalupe. In the aftermath of the attack, Garraleta could have run down the Hutnyilshs on horseback while they were on foot, but he chose to stay at the mission and do nothing (Rojo [1879] 1972).

Hutnyilsh retired to Los Alamos, on the bottom of Nejí Canyon. He was interviewed late in life regarding the events at Mission Guadalupe and Father Félix Caballero:

My name is Hutnyilsh, and I have been the chief of this tribe since the year in which Lieutenant Ruiz left here for the South (1822); my father was chief before me, and before my father, my grandfather; so that the command of our tribe was always in the hands of my family, and that's why the tribe bears my own name. My father used to tell me that this land would belong to the *gente de razón* and for me not to go against them, just as he and my grandfather were not against them; we were always friends of the white men, and we, like them, don't like robbery and don't like to kill anyone without a reason. I helped Father

Caballero build Mission El Descanso from its foundation
to the end; I don't remember any more when this was
(1830); shortly afterwards I went out to campaign with
Macedonio González against the Indians of Santa Catarina, the [Kiliwa], and the [Cocopah], who at that time
were very numerous; a thousand warriors followed my
orders, and with all my men I fought all the time against
those tribes who killed the majority of my best warriors;
we killed a lot of them too. . . . We kept fighting for more
than a year, until all the tribes in revolt were pacified; and
then I came to help Father Félix raise Mission Guadalupe from its foundations to the end, and I also helped
him to sow every year and to harvest his crops; and the
father used to give us what he wanted to—corn, barley,
and wheat, from that which we ourselves had sowed and
harvested but, not content with this, he tried to get us to
be baptized several times in order to have us shut up in the
mission and handle us like the rest of the Indians; after I
saved the escort which went into the Jacumé Mountains
with Macedonio González when Pedro Pablo, Martín,
and Cartucho rebelled, I left the coast range because
there were many enemies there who could attack me, and
I came to make my fort at a watering place on the table
land of El Descanso, very suitable for defending ourselves
because the place on which it is looks like a fort; Father
Félix surely thought that I wouldn't be able to go back
to the mountain out of fear, and that I was very weak so
that he could do what he wanted with me and my people;
and then, without remembering my services and the fact
that all our labors stemmed from having wanted to help
the *gente de razón*, against the will of all of us he began
to baptize by force the people of my tribe who went to

visit him as we were accustomed to doing; this made me very angry and for that reason I went to look for him in Guadalupe with the intention of killing him; I didn't want to kill or harm anyone but him, but the people I took with me got ahead of me while I stopped a while in the mountain; it was they who, without orders from me, killed Corporal Orantes and the Indians Francisco and José Antonio. After I arrived nobody did anything, and since I didn't find Father Félix I left the mission again and we didn't take anything from it. After that, I returned to this settlement and I haven't gone anywhere. Look, I can't even see from old age; most of my people died in the war; others became excited and went to Upper California at the time of the placer mines and haven't returned; so, you see, I only have a few families left and we all work without stealing from anyone. (Rojo [1879] 1972)

———

Father Caballero knew he was a hunted man. He got no support from the soldiers who were behaving coolly and indifferently toward him after the Guadalupe attack. So he didn't even bother to collect all his personal possessions and livestock but left as quickly as possible for the Mission San Vicente just outside of the Kumeyaay lands. From there he went to the Mission San Ignacio in Cochimí territory to settle down. On August 3, 1840, six months after the Guadalupe attack, Father Caballero was drinking a cup of chocolate as he did every day after saying mass. This day, however, he began to feel sharp pains in his stomach as though he were poisoned. He died a few hours later. No charges were ever brought for his death. The Mission San Ignacio was abandoned later that year.

Whether such was the reach of Hutnyilsh (over four hundred miles from Kumeyaay lands), or whether another enemy of Father

Caballero had found his target is unknown. We do know that the desire of the Mexicans to placate Hutnyilsh during this time of uprisings was clearly in recognition of his military strength. We also know that this would not be the first time that Kumeyaay had resorted to poisoning a priest to exact justice: in November 1811 Nazario, a neophyte cook, was arrested and tried for the attempted murder of Father José Pedro Panto. According to the records, Nazario poisoned Panto's soup with powdered *cuchasquelaai*, a type of yerba, in revenge for repeated severe beatings. In his defense of Nazario, the public defender, José Mario Pico, urged that the Indian be acquitted because the poison was not fatal and the beatings—fifty, twenty-five, twenty-four, and twenty-five lashes (*azotes*) over a twenty-four hour period just preceding the poisoning—were unjustified. The prosecutor, Domingo Carrillo, agreed in spirit but stated that other Indians must be warned that such actions would not be tolerated and successfully argued for eight months of labor at the presidio as a penalty. Pedro Panto died seven months later of what appeared to be the effects of the poisoning (Carrico 1990).

Hutnyilsh removed his protections from the Dominican missions, and within a short time Missions San Miguel, Guadalupe, and Descanso were destroyed. Hutnyilsh went on to live a long life as a non-Christian. It is said that he allowed himself to be baptized on his deathbed.

Indian people had many approaches to surviving the entry of the Spanish colonial mission system into California. For Hutnyilsh and his people, a secular alliance with the Spanish provided access to their material goods while preserving traditional culture and religion. For many Indigenous peoples in California, such an agreement would have been impossible to negotiate. The conditions were enhanced for the Hutnyilshs by the Dominicans' fear after the destruction of Mission San Diego by the Kumeyaay and the missions on the Colorado River by the Quechan. Governor Fages's directive to avoid antagonizing the local Indians also played a major role. Most *sh'mulls* numbered around two hundred people before the coming of the Europeans. For Hutnyilsh to have one thousand warriors meant a total population of potentially three thousand or more persons from several *sh'mulls* at his greatest strength. This would have made the Hutnyilsh Nation the strongest of any of the recorded Kumeyaay coalitions. Descendants of Hutnyilsh reside on the Indigenous *ejidos* of Juntas de Nejí and San Jose de la Zorra in Baja California.

The story of the Hutnyilshs is just one example of the wide range of Native adaptation to the occupation of their lands by Spanish and Mexican colonialists. It also illustrates that the Spaniards and Mexicans were not adverse to accommodating Native culture and beliefs, at least for a time, if it served their primary goals of domination. It is ironic that the longest and strongest alliance between the colonial missions and the Kumeyaay was one that specifically excluded Christianity.

WE ARE STILL HERE

DEBORAH DOZIER

*T*he following text is from a conversation that took place in July
1991, primarily between the author and the Cahuilla elder
Katherine Siva Saubel (1920–2011). Saubel cofounded and was president
of Malki Museum, which focuses on Cahuilla culture and is based on
Morongo Reservation. The books she authored include I'isniyatam
(An Interpretation of Cahuilla Designs); Chem'ivillu' (Let's Speak
Cahuilla); *and, with Lowell J. Bean,* Temalpakh (From the Earth),
*an ethnobotanical work for Southern California. She was a major
contributor to the* Cahuilla Dictionary, *published by Malki Museum in
1979. Among the many awards and honors she received in her lifetime,
she was one of the first people to be awarded by the National Museum
of the American Indian for her culture work. Also participating in this
conversation were Dolores (Dee) Alvarez, independent businesswoman
and past director of education for Soboba Band of Mission Indians;
Anthony "Biff" Andreas, past vice-chair and tribal historian at Agua
Caliente Reservation; and JoMay Modesto, independent businesswoman
and administrator in various roles at Cahuilla Reservation.*

Katherine Siva Saubel: When the first Spaniards landed in the territory, the Indian people were looking at them and were afraid of them. They thought they were ghosts. They thought the Spanish were dead people because they looked so white; they needed blood, they were dying people. Here they were, the conquerors, you know, they were coming in and the Cahuilla didn't want to go near them because they thought they had some kind of disease, see? That's what the Indians said when they were looking at them. But it wasn't that way at all. The Spanish were here to get what they were going to get from us—and they did.

The Cahuilla were afraid of them. Not only then but after a while because of the way they were treated. They were pushed out of their land and they were afraid. They didn't have no rights in their own land. They lost everything. I think that was just the beginning of the end of my people.

And then after a while some Cahuillas tried to learn the Spanish language and they did go to work for a lot of Spaniards that had the big ranches here. They went to work for them, either to take care of their cows and horses, like cowboys, or to work their fields, whatever jobs they could get. Some of them had to go from their traditional homes to shear the lambs at the times when they had to be sheared. They got jobs like that. Any job they could get. That's what they did afterwards.

And then after the Spanish, the Mexicans came. The Mexicans were kind of a little bit lenient to the Indian because they, the Mexicans, were Indian too. The Spanish conquered them and so they had a little bit of compassion for the Indian and tried to give some portions of land—not little portions, but big portions—to the Indian people. But before the Mexicans completed the giving, the Anglos took over. They were just as bad as the Spanish. They were just there to destroy the Indians.

40

That's when we really became, you might say, beggars, because we had no place to hunt, no place to gather anymore. We were just held down to the different areas. Sometimes to areas where we didn't even belong—we were moved around by whoever was in power. It was really a trauma for my people. They became so, how would you say . . . They were always hungry now, they were always in a sad situation. I guess they just had to live with what little they could get just to survive. But they were really destroyed.

When they [the Americans] came, we Cahuilla were really just ignored for quite, I think, a long time. In fact, they just wanted to clear us off the area. I think that's why most of the time, my people, the Cahuillas, were afraid to go anywhere. They were safer in their own areas. Those were in the interior part, and I think that's why we are still here today—on account of that geographic situation. Otherwise, we would have been like the coastal Indians. They were destroyed right away. Their culture was ruined. Like the Chumash, the Gabrielinos, and all that.

Deborah Dozier: Was it the American government that took the Cupeños out of Warner Springs?

KSS: I don't really understand that at all. I know that when the Indians were going to be taken off their land . . . the Americans said that area was being given to Jack Warner. One of the Spanish land grants went to him. The Indians never knew anything about Spanish land grants. They knew it was their land, they were living there. But the Americans had already given that land to Warner without the knowledge of the Indian people. And when they came to remove them, they just removed them by force.

DD: What did they do?

KSS: My father was telling me—he was there, and this is what he saw. When they came there he said they just brought this long band of wagons, and they just threw the Indians' belongings in there, and I guess just actually put the people on there by force. And a lot of the people were crying. Everybody was crying. A lot of the old people ran off into the hills. A lot of them were never seen again.

DD: Where were they taking them on these wagons?

KSS: They had to take them from Warner Springs to Pala. They had to go by the road that goes out to Temecula and then turns left into Pala. And that's quite a ways. I don't know how long it took them, but it probably had to take them maybe a day, two days, or three days to get over there.

DD: Why were they taking them there?

KSS: That's one of the things too. The Indians had their own boundary lines, and the people at Warner's were taken into the Luiseños' territory. And a lot of those Indians from Warner's didn't want to go there because it was not their area. But the white man didn't care about that, didn't care that they had their own areas where they lived. So they forced them over there to live with the Luiseños. I heard the Luiseños were very offended because the Americans didn't tell them anything over there either, they just walked them in there. Because they were Indians, they didn't care where they put them. But the Indian is not that way. He has his own villages, his own areas. That was disruptive when they were moved.

DD: Tell me about the smallpox epidemics.

KSS: It's really one of the things that destroyed the Cahuilla people, I believe. I think at that time, smallpox was introduced to the Cahuilla people deliberately. They wanted to get rid of us. They deliberately sent those blankets and things like that infected with smallpox to the Indian people. At that time, when the Cahuillas got that disease, almost seventy percent maybe, more or less, died out because they didn't know about the disease. That's what killed them off. That just really reduced us—besides going hungry and not having our own areas anymore. We were really, really devastated by the smallpox.

DD: What's the implication of having seventy percent of your population gone?

KSS: Well, to me . . . When I asked my father that, I said, "The white man said we were about five thousand or whatever, six thousand here." He said, "No, there were more than that." He said at that time there were about fifteen thousand. The way he said it, it was about fifteen thousand. Maybe more, he said, because we were so widespread, [it was] a long territory that the Cahuilla lived in. There was a lot of people at one time. Each village had one or two hundred people. There was a lot of villages. There must have been that much, that's what he said.

DD: What happens to your social structure, your religious structure, your economic structure, when seventy percent of your people are gone?

KSS: We really lost all of our economic way of things that we had here. Before contact, my father said every person never went hungry. They had food here, they had wild berries, they had acorns, they had things that they could use. They had lots of game here. The antelopes were still here. The bighorns, the deer, the rabbit. And so he said we always had food. And then when the Anglos came, they lost all that and they got hungry. In a lot of pictures you will see now where they look so ragged and everything else. That's on account of that. Everything was destroyed and they couldn't use this or that. I think that's the time when some of them, I believe, would just give up.

What really surprised me was when they made the treaties with the Indians here at that time, in the 1850s, and they promised so many things that they were supposed to give them—large parcels of land where they could live, not just like five acres like they have now. I think it was supposed to be 160 acres, or so many acres to the families. But that never happened. Of course, those treaties were never ratified by the Congress, so the Indians never got the land that was given to them. Finally, in the late, I think, 1880s or '90s, they set aside the reservations. The Indians used to live up there where the town is now. On the side there [indicating a 270° arc] and over here. They were moved over here, all around here. The land they were moved from was taken over years ago. And who could they appeal to? They didn't have no voice anywhere. The Indians couldn't say anything against the white man. He had all the rights. The Indian had nothing. So they just went down and lost everything.

DD: Fifty years ago Perfecto Segundo, a venerated shaman, predicted the end of Cahuilla culture as it was.[1] Do you think there will be a Cahuilla culture five hundred years from now?

KSS: I doubt it. I doubt it very much. Because in the first place, the Cahuilla are terminating themselves even from being Cahuilla, by intermarriage. I think that is one of the things that is going to take away from who we are, especially the Cahuilla.

---

[1] In the early 1930s Perfecto Segundo said, "There was a lot of Indian people here at one time. There is no more. No place is theirs anymore in these effigy ceremonies. There is no longer any other dances, ceremonial dances. There is no eagle dance. Nothing is there anymore. Now that is gone. That is all.

"The kids, the children that are left now will never know what it was. This is the way it will be, this is the way it is. It is finished. It is already done. It is understood. We do not know what it will be now. Everything is disappearing. I am the one that is talking now, Perfecto Segundo. I am seventy-four years old. That is why I am saying this."

From the beginning, the Cahuilla people always followed the father's line. And now, if the father is not Cahuilla, where is the line? There will be other Indians, I suppose, in five hundred years, but I don't think there will be any Cahuilla.

And that is if we live that long. If we are not poisoned out. All of us, not just Cahuillas. Well, I think the only way we can do that now is to train the children. The children, I think, are the ones that can grow up to be who they are . . . if we instruct them in the right way. I think they can still retain some part of it when they get older. Otherwise, without them, we are going to be gone.

DD: How do you feel about the culture disappearing?

KSS: Well, I feel bad about it, because it is happening now in my lifetime. I have seen a lot of changes. I have rode in the wagons a long time ago before I knew the car. I never knew the car until I moved to Palm Springs. All these things that we used a long time ago, from that time on up to the cars, and then when I found out about the trains, and about the airplanes and everything else—it is just going, going, going. There are more different changes now, like to outer space. We are the ones that are really going to be gone. The ones that lived on this continent. The first inhabitants.

DD: What do we lose if Indian culture disappears?

KSS: The worst thing I worry about is the land itself. The white man is destroying himself with all his nuclear powers and this and that. Look at how many people are fighting against the nuclear things over here in the Nevada desert. It is going to be all over pretty soon. It will probably be all over. And things like that, the people . . . this is not going to be just right here, it will be all over the world. Look at that Chernobyl, at whatever happened there. It is still going through killing a lot of people. Even into Sweden and all those places. It is just not in that one area, it goes all over. We may not be here in five hundred years, the way things are going.

Indian culture, I think, was the only way to live with the respect of everything around you. Respect yourself and the people. Really get along, try to live in peace, and to preserve this land. The land is the most important thing you can think of. Without that, you are nothing.

DD: What is being done to preserve Cahuilla culture?

KSS: I read that book on Palm Springs that Francisco Patencio wrote [*Stories and Legends of the Palm Springs Indians*]. In the front part he said this was written for the children that are to come because they won't know anymore. I think that is important to talk about. But we have to explain a lot of it. We have to explain who we are and where we are coming from. It encompasses all of those things, to show exactly where we are at, so they realize and appreciate, and to get the ideas across that we want to show them—all kinds of things. But if they don't understand where we are coming from, it is pointless.

Dolores (Dee) Alvarez: I think that a lot of it has to do with the work that Lowell [Bean] has done and the people that he has worked with, to bring that awareness back. They said we were "digger" Indians. It was like you were animals. You dug here, you dug there. Then I found out that we owned property. We own property here, we own property there. We had our own roads. I learned all this from what they said. There was a purpose for it all, it wasn't just because you were going to own and acquire, the materialist kind of stuff. It wasn't that at all.

What I can see is men, it would have been the men, sitting around and discussing how something was going to work. The things that you did, like disposing of your fingernails and your hair. That was all ecology, to keep things clean. Everything that they thought about was for a reason and a purpose. I find it really fascinating that they thought that far ahead, like playing chess. These intelligent people had a system that worked out far better than what the Plains had.

JoMay Modesto: Well, I think a long time ago—even, let's say, with my grandmother—that the culture changed. They had to change from the beads to money, the shell money, and then it went to contemporary money. When we went to using the material, everything was replaced.

Change has always been something that Cahuillas have had to do to survive. To accept that . . . to change and to constantly go figure out, "How much do I give, how do I really want to share?" You change, you end up doing it because that means survival of the people.

DA: I think it had a lot of effect on their self-esteem when men had to go out to work and make a living for their families because the land wasn't there to be used. They may have been that powerful person, important person, in their clan and with their family. And then when they get out and they are working for this white, rich farmer it was going to be racial and degrading, and I think that is why a lot of them started drinking. They couldn't handle it. The woman, being still in the house, was protected from having to get out there.

DD: How did the Malki Museum get started?

KSS: Jane Penn started that. She had left here when she was a young girl, a teenager, in fact. She must have been about sixteen or seventeen. She went to live in Los Angeles. She worked and lived in Los Angeles. Then she came home when she was forty-nine years old. When she came back she realized that all the people that lived here were gone, the older people. She just had her cousin and her aunt living. She talked to her cousin, saying that they had given her some artifacts of theirs, her cousin. She said she should start something to save all this. She said there was nobody around anymore and we should have something. She spoke to Lowell Bean, and he is the one who helped her to get all of us together and we started that museum. On a shoestring—we didn't have any money at all. That was in 1963. There was a lot of them that helped us out that were non-Indians.

The Malki Museum is one of the nice things that happened to the Indian people, because that is holding things there that was just the remnants of what we used to be, what the Cahuilla culture was in the past. That is the only place where the Indian fifty or sixty years from now can find out who they were, what language they spoke. Everything is there. I think it is just like a library or something for the Indian. Not only the Indian, but the non-Indian that wants to learn about us. We have had a lot of scholars working there with us to find out about different things. I think it is something that really helps the people understand who was here and what they had done.

DD: Tell me about the Malki Museum Press.

KSS: We realized that a lot of things were being lost. We also realized that the books that were written about the Cahuilla, or about any Indian for that matter, were written by non-Indians. It was never from our point of view, it was from theirs all the time. At Malki Press, a lot of Indian authors speak as Indian people. So I think that is one of the things that is really interesting to me. That we can do that, you know, have our own press.

We have some Indian authors published by Malki Press that put down their own recollections . . . like when I was about twelve or thirteen years old, when I spoke Cahuilla to my peers, my own people that went to school with me, they would answer me in English all the time. I talked to them in my language. That's when I realized that the language is going to go right away, because they don't want to talk it. They understood every bit of it, they could speak it at that time, but they were no longer using it. That is why

I worked on the dictionary of our language.

Then I realized, too, that the plants and things we used, what our people were doctored with, that was disappearing. That's why I helped to write this book [*Temalpakh*] about the plants. Because I know that nobody else is going to use them. I knew a lot of this from my mother's side. That's why I started to keep a notebook, when I was in high school, of the plants and things like that. When I met Dr. Bean, I showed him that notebook. I said, "Can we do something about this?" He said, "Yes, we will work on it. I will supply all the Latin names and you will supply the Indian names." With his help I worked on that book. I thought that was one of the best things that we did.

DD: How many volumes has the Malki Press published?

KSS: We have already published about maybe thirty-two or thirty-three different books. We have one on the line right now, the medicine book of the Chumash people [*Chumash Healing*, by Philip L. Walker and Travis Hudson, published in 1993]. After that, we have another book to publish. That will be a big book with a lot of pictures. This is the Tongva or Gabrielino book [*The First Angelinos*, by William McCawley, published in 1996].

DD: Now the Agua Caliente Band has plans to construct a cultural center/museum in Palm Springs?

Anthony Andreas: Yes. We hope it will be open in 1995.[2] It will be a museum of Agua Caliente history and an archive for bird song recordings. It will also have a space where we put up temporary exhibitions about other Indians. We have worked with many different people to plan the most modern museum possible. We hope to be accredited by the American Association of Museums. You have to be a really good museum to do that.

It is one way we can save the bird songs. I don't know if the younger generations will know the bird songs completely. That's another reason we are trying to build this museum in Palm Springs. To have things that our younger kids can learn from and see, because we are not close anymore. We are so separated. That is nobody's fault. That is just the way things are, the way things happen. And this museum would bring everybody together to know their history. Even if they don't know the language, at least they will know the history, and "This is my great-grandfather, my great-grandmother. These songs, so-and-so sang them, that is my great-uncle." They would have that sense of pride. It will make them proud, even if they don't talk the language or sing the songs. That history part is very important.

DD: What are the challenges facing the Cahuilla as the culture moves into the future?

KSS: Years ago the non-Indian came in here. Since then we have always had the problem. I call it the White problem, but everybody else calls it the Indian problem. It is not that. We never had a problem here until the non-Indian got here, then we had problems. So it is not the Indian problem as far as the Indian is concerned [laughs].

I don't know what will be. The only thing I want is for them to leave us alone so we can live in peace. We don't bother anybody. But it just doesn't seem that way. Too many unscrupulous developers. Too many of them are greedy people, and that's what is destroying us—greed.

I hope our message goes through, that what we are doing will open up the eyes of the public to what's happening, what is going on today. The federal government is trying to allow the people to

---

[2] The Agua Caliente Cultural Center in Palm Springs.

put toxic wastes in the reservations. When you are trying to preserve your way of life, your culture and everything, trying to save what little you have, if you don't have any more land, what are you going to do? Nothing. See, there is no more. That is the ending of it.

I think there is a purpose to all of this. From the beginning, there was genocide, like smallpox, and then killing the Indians in central California by poisoning them, and things like that. But we were so strong, we just hung on. We're *here*. But that's the whole purpose— to get rid of us, as you know. I never read it in history books, but the idea of the President, Andrew Jackson, was to annihilate us from the face of the earth—to kill us, hunt us like animals. Each head fifty dollars or five dollars, whatever. That's the whole thing.

They find all different ways to do that—the Allotment Act, the Termination Act, all these different acts. They were not going to help the Indians. They are going to destroy us.

But it is still going on, like I said. Now they are still continuing genocide at the present time with the toxic waste and garbage things on our reservations. And that is going to destroy us, because it is going to destroy the land, the water, the air, everything around us.

JM: Protecting the land is really hard. Even with the rock art, if we were to protect everything, we would have to protect from the desert to wherever our territory was. No matter what you are into, you are going to find something, some artifact, something. There is always a turmoil, all the time—what to do with it.

DA: There are a lot of caves where there are spearheads or flints and prehistoric animals in this area, Southern California. A lot of those areas are where Indians probably lived. The evidence they are finding now is just recent, two to three thousand years.

We found an arrowhead when we were doing our tribal hall. The archeological report said it was six thousand years old. It was on top of the ground. They were just walking across and found it.

They sent that one to Washington for dating. They sent it back to us. It was kind of sad, because here is this person who just sent it off. We didn't even know it was gone. When it came back it was kind of weird. We opened the package up at the tribal hall during a meeting and here it had gone so far and been away so long. But they gave it back and we did what we wanted to do with it. We reburied it.

When we did something, it was taken care of at that time. Six thousand years later, we have to deal with this arrowhead that we had. We chose to rebury it. We don't know how to do the ceremonies anymore. The ceremonies protect us. If we don't do it right, then it will come back to us. You are always in a conflict with yourself and the reality of what you are dealing with. It is really difficult to have to go through all of these things.

KSS: So when an arrowhead or rock art is found, what are we going to do with it? We don't know who made those. Whatever the power in those rocks, it is still there. Whether it will hurt us if we touch it and we take it to our home or we take it to a museum we don't know, because we don't have the shamans anymore. They are the ones that know.

We may have the shamans. Their power probably came to them and talked to them, but it talked to them in Indian and they didn't understand what the power was saying. This is the problem now.

You are born with the power. It comes to you very young. And it may come to you when you are older, but you have to recognize it. You have to be an Indian to recognize it. If you are an Indian in just name, you don't understand what he is saying. So you just ignore it, so it either leaves you or it is there, but you don't know what to do with it.

I guess that is why my brother Cruz said, "We are lost. Nobody knows, we might as well forget it." But, you cannot forget it. You are an Indian, and whatever is going to affect you is not going to say, "Well, you don't speak Indian anymore so I won't bother you." He says, "You are an Indian, and I am going to kill you." And that is what they will do.

So you can't forget it. I don't know how much Indian you have to have in you before it leaves—how much other blood besides Indian—before it leaves you—but if you are Indian, it is there for you.

SPEAKING OUT: RUPERT COSTO AND THE AMERICAN INDIAN HISTORICAL SOCIETY

ROSE SOZA WAR SOLDIER

I n 1964 the iconic Ford Mustang rolled off the assembly line, the hot and violent Freedom Summer resulted in voter registration throughout the South, Congress passed the Civil Rights Act, the Free Speech Movement started at UC Berkeley, Beatlemania began, Dr. Martin Luther King Jr. received the Nobel Peace Prize, Malcolm X delivered his speech "The Ballot or the Bullet," and President Lyndon Johnson declared a War on Poverty. In addition, the San Francisco–based American Indian Historical Society (AIHS or simply the Society) formally incorporated under the leadership of Rupert Costo (Cahuilla). The organization worked to cultivate mutual understanding between Indians and non-Indians. The Society believed it would be able to defend and advocate for Indian self-determination through education and the creation of a shared knowledge base.

Bibliographic references for this essay can be found in the References and Notes section at the back of the book.

The AIHS worked to improve education, communication, and cultural development among Indians. Members of this activist organization challenged textbooks, testified at congressional hearings, created an Indian-controlled publishing house, coordinated community meetings, and lobbied for protection of burial grounds. It also circulated *Wassaja*, one of the first national Indian newspapers with original content. The AIHS philosophy centered on the belief that Indians could, through their own initiative and innovation, lead the fight in Indian affairs. Through the years, the Society supported Indian issues and the efforts of individual tribes to preserve their rights.

Some ambiguity surrounds the origins of the AIHS. The only president, Rupert Costo, and his wife, Jeannette Henry-Costo (Eastern Cherokee), worked on historical research prior to the formal incorporation in 1964. According to Costo, it began as "mostly a family research endeavor at first, building up a library, writing articles, doing research" (Hillinger 1977). The Costos publicly credited the suggestion to their personal friend Dr. George Hammond, who they met while conducting research at UC Berkeley's Bancroft Library, where he was the director at the time (Costo and Henry-Costo 1995, ix).[1] The AIHS recognized his contribution by unanimously selecting him as one of the first consulting members to the organization.

The Society eventually claimed hundreds of members, but a core group, representing the diversity of the Indian community in California and across Indian Country, regularly worked on issues. The

---

[1] However, in AIHS meeting minutes from July 25, 1964, Costo asserted the idea for the organization originated from his private organization The Indian Archives. In a 1966 reprinted speech before the California League for American Indians, Costo asserted the formal AIHS organization emerged as an outgrowth of the Indian Library and Archives, founded by a small group of Cahuillas about twenty-five years previously to help them with their litigation against the federal government (Costo 1966, 14).

Costos formally established the Society with tribal members from Choctaw, Klamath, and several California Indian tribes, including Cahuilla, Karuk, Me-wuk, Tolowa, and Quechan (American Indian Historical Society 1964b). The initial fifteen-member board of directors included four tribal chairpersons: Rupert Costo of the Cahuilla reservation; Edmond Jackson, Yuma of the Fort Yuma reservation; Emmett St. Marie, Cahuilla of the Morongo reservation; and George Wessell, Me-wuk of the Tuolumne rancheria. Additionally, six women served on the original board of directors: Viola Fuller Wessell (Me-wuk); Sylvia Green (Tolowa); Jeannette Henry-Costo; Nancy Landuck (Karuk); Jane Penn (Cahuilla); and Bertha Stewart (Tolowa). Stewart served as vice president for the first few years. Membership on the board of directors occasionally changed and individuals from the Blackfoot, Maidu, Navajo, Ohlone, Paiute, Pueblo, Inupiat, Yakima, and Yurok tribes also contributed during the formative early years of the organization.

The board of directors represented the broad diversity of Indians living in California. The members' ages generally ranged from mid-forties to mid-sixties, with the youngest, San Francisco State student Robert "Bob" Kaniatobe (Choctaw), in his late twenties. Several of the founding board members or their families had also participated in earlier California organizations, including the California Indian Rights Association and Federated Indians of California.

At an AIHS board of directors meeting on July 14, 1964, the organization formulated its purpose:

> 1. To study, interpret and disclose the facts concerning the history of the American Indians, to preserve and protect the remaining evidence of Indian customs, arts, and cultures, and to correct the historical record as to the true story of the Indians and their contributions to civilization.

2. To inform and educate the public at large concerning the history of the American Indians.

3. To work for the education, the good and welfare, and the cultural development of the American Indians.

4. Agreed that the organization must be nonprofit absolutely, and that the organization be nonpolitical absolutely. (American Indian Historical Society 1964a)

The AIHS committed to cultivating cultural unity among Indians, not cultural uniformity. It strived for respect and mutual understanding among tribal nations. As a result, the organization stressed tribal issues, rejected a broad pan-Indian identity, and insisted on preserving distinct tribal identities. Indeed, Costo described the attempts at pan-Indianism as a "historic extermination." Costo strongly believed any attempts at pan-Indian identity must be rejected because of the danger it posed to tribal culture. He explained, "I am afraid of this kind of unity which is based on smoothing out cultural differences will destroy us quicker than the efforts at assimilation have done so far" (Costo 1967, 2). The AIHS embraced cohesion, solidarity, and unity based on common goals. In part, the formal headquarters located in San Francisco facilitated the organization's success because of its central location and supportive environment.

The Costos held Society meetings in their home at first; however, in 1966 the group sought a site where they could establish a national headquarters with space for meetings, a library, and an art museum. Jeannette Henry-Costo and Bertha Stewart found a Victorian two-story built in 1900, with an attic and nine rooms. Located at 1451 Masonic Avenue, between Golden Gate Park and Buena Vista Park, it is less than half a mile south of the iconic Haight and Ashbury intersection, known for its hippie subculture in the 1960s.

Establishing the AIHS headquarters at that location required approval from the San Francisco City Planning Commission, which voted unanimously for approval against the advice of Acting Zoning Administrator Robert Passmore. Arguments opposing the location included concern about nighttime meetings, parking, and fears that its establishment would encourage commercial development. However, Commissioner James Kearney noted, "I think they [the AIHS] will improve and stabilize the neighborhood." He continued, "I think this is one of the nicest things that could happen there." Additionally, James Brown, president of the Haight-Ashbury Neighborhood Council, endorsed the AIHS location and declared "We welcome diversity. It adds a yeast to our neighborhood that we encourage" ("Indians among the Hippies" 1967, 4). On May 6, 1967, the headquarters, known as Chautauqua House, opened its doors. AIHS members and their families diligently worked on updating and cleaning the house in preparation for its opening. Those highlighted for their work included Don and Dallas Hammond; Philip, Sara, Michael, Eleanor, and Andy Galvan; Dolores and Mannie LaMeira; and Darrell and Becky Hylton ("The Chautauqua Spokesman" 1967, 2). An announcement for the opening of the AIHS headquarters, which highlighted the inaugural museum exhibition of paintings by father and son Carl and Rudolph Gorman (Navajo), appeared in the *San Francisco Chronicle* ("Indian Society" 1967).

The most visible political activity that occurred near the AIHS headquarters took place in November 1969 with the occupation of Alcatraz Island. As residents of San Francisco, the Costos were aware of the Alcatraz occupation but did not participate in it. The organization discussed Alcatraz, with "no action taken" (American Indian Historical Society 1969). Indeed, some members viewed the occupation critically because they were displeased with out-of-state Indians claiming the historic homelands of the Ohlone. Costo acknowledged that the occupation had support from the general public, which could translate into additional support for other issues raised by Indians. However, he questioned the efficiency of the occupation and the significant number of college-age participants. He believed that by leaving school for the occupation, college students jeopardized newly established Native American studies programs (Costo 1970, 11). Some California Indians stood apart from Alcatraz, while others fully participated in the occupation.

The Galvan family had several family members active in the AIHS. Felipe "Philip" Galvan (Ohlone) served as the secretary of the Society. Upset about the Alcatraz occupation, Galvan and other Ohlones expressed their concern by submitting a petition to President Richard Nixon. The petition letter, dated January 22, 1970, explained that although Indians on Alcatraz claimed to speak for all Indians, "they do not," and informed the president that no participants of Alcatraz had any authority to speak on behalf of the Ohlones. The letter called the occupation "wrong" and suggested Alcatraz activists "are mainly from other states, other tribes and reservations." By pointing out many of the Alcatraz activists were from outside of California, and describing historic Ohlone home-lands "from Pleasanton in the East Bay to the Coast, and southerly to Monterey, including the islands along the coast," the Ohlones supported their claim that if any Indians had a right to claim Alcatraz, they did (Ohlone Indians of California 1970).

The Society committed to supporting Ohlone self-determination. Costo publicly criticized American Indian Movement (AIM) co-founder Dennis Banks (Ojibwa) for prematurely taking up the issue of Indian remains and artifacts found in San Jose at a Holiday Inn garage construction site "on behalf" of Ohlones without their knowledge or informed consent. Galvan remarked on Banks's lack of consultation with the Ohlones, noting, "Neither Banks nor any other Indian speaks for the Ohlone Indians." Costo expressed full support for Galvan and the Ohlone. Costo recognized the challenge of Indians from various tribes moving to California with good intentions, but sometimes intruding on local Indigenous communities' issues. Costo commented on Banks's actions, noting "That's not his business. . . . This is not a question of fancy-stepping protocol. It is tribal sovereignty." Costo acknowledged supporting Banks's earlier causes, but concluded Banks needed to "back off" on interjecting himself (Costo 1977, 2). The Ohlones, according to Costo, had previously consulted with builders and worked to re-inter their ancestral remains and did not require external assistance.

In addition to supporting tribal self-determination, the Society placed a priority on correcting misinformation and stereotypes in history textbooks used in California's public schools. One of the earliest AIHS activities included examining and evaluating textbooks used in elementary and middle schools, which were some of the earliest evaluations of California Indian depictions in textbooks used in public schools. The AIHS considered the form and content of history education significant for several reasons. For serious discussions of policy to occur, misconceptions about Indian cultures, traditions, and historical experiences had to be deconstructed and addressed. Public opinion informed political policy, and if Indians and Indigenous cultures appeared as caricatures, any possible shift in policy would be even more difficult to achieve. Some textbooks simply failed to mention Indians. The absence of Indians in textbooks silently equated Indians as a culture either historically insignificant or, perhaps, a population completely destroyed in the past, and therefore not worthy of mention. In addition, by confronting history textbook content and imagery, the AIHS hoped to shift the negative self-perception of Indian students exposed to Indian caricatures in textbooks.

The AIHS had specific interest in public schools because the overwhelming majority of Indian students in California attended public schools in the aftermath of the 1924 *Piper* decision. However, it is difficult to determine if public school attendance translated into quality education and equal treatment. A report completed by the Commonwealth Club of California in 1926 detailed responses to Indian children enrolling at public schools ranging from "cruel exploitation" to "friendliness and honesty." The report shared the story of Middle Creek District in Lake County. Due to the closure of an Indian day school, the public school accepted fourteen Indian students, but partitioned off a special room, fenced in a section of the playground, and hired a separate teacher for them (Drew 1926, 115). Thus, *de facto* segregation and mistreatment of Indian students continued despite changes in the law.

The AIHS created the Indian History Study Committee in 1965 to review textbooks. Chaired by Costo, the committee included Henry Azbill (Maidu), Edna Calac (Pit River), Martina Costo (Cahuilla), Jeannette Henry-Costo, Laura Dusney (Karuk), Erin Forrest (Pit River), Richard Fuller (Me-wuk), Al Hicks (Navajo), Edmond Jackson (Quechan), Wallace Newman (Luiseño), Marie Potts (Maidu), Bertha Stewart (Tolowa), Viola Fuller Wessell (Me-wuk), and Thelma Wilson (Maidu) ("Education Study Begins" 1965). The committee greatly benefited from the participation of two teachers, Martina Costo and Al Hicks, who provided practical insight. It worked on developing curriculum criteria for the California Curriculum Commission and Board of Education to consult. As a result, those responsible for the process of California textbook selection became better informed on the depiction and representation of Indians.

In addition to reviewing textbooks, the Society secured a grant from the Rosenberg Foundation, a group established in 1935 and dedicated to the welfare of California children, for direct outreach to public schools and teachers. According to the 1965 Rosenberg report, the AIHS was the first all-Indian organization to approach the foundation. The Society received a grant of $9,987 to create and sponsor a program to make more accurate information on Indians available in public schools (American Indian Historical Society 1965). In 1966, the AIHS held five workshops, called "Program of Indian

Aid to Education," across the state in Berkeley, Beaumont, Fresno, Hoopa, and San Francisco. Speaking about the Berkeley workshop, Henry-Costo commented, "We want to change the public's image of the Indian as a quaint, out-of-the-world character and show him as he is—a live wire in today's world" ("Workshop on Indian at Berkeley" 1966). Ultimately, over 1,652 educators attended the workshops. They returned to their classrooms with materials, teaching guides, and direct positive interaction with Indians.

For a number of years, the AIHS worked toward correcting history textbooks used in public schools and to reflect the experiences of Indians by eliminating one-dimensional caricatures. However, after years of working toward this goal with California state officials and publishing houses, the AIHS decided that if published items did not properly represent Indians, then it would create and distribute its own materials. By responding in this manner, the Society offered an alternative to Indian peoples being ignored or misrepresented and provided an opportunity for Indians to assert their own voices.

The Society recognized the potential imbued in the written word and its circulation. In the aftermath of earlier government policies of genocide and relocating for economic opportunities, the dramatically decreased California Indian population was scattered across the state. The written, published word served as a powerful tool, reconnecting and facilitating a network of writers, scholars, artists, and activists in California and across Indian Country. The AIHS created publications parallel to mainstream media for both general readers and the scholarly community, and sought to reveal the humanity and cultural diversity of Indians. The publications shaped a sense of community between and among reservation and urban Indians as they developed a cultural belonging through common readership.

The Society represented the ongoing tradition of multitribal organizational activism among California Indians. Their members believed they had a responsibility to advocate for the betterment of the people and practiced solidarity around common goals. California's eighteen un-ratified treaties served as a central rallying point and encouraged the establishment of California Indian organizations throughout the twentieth century. Thus, organizational activism is a historic cultural practice among California Indians.

The story of the AIHS demonstrates the diversity of activism and advocacy during the 1960s and 1970s. Costo encouraged controversy and took glee in it. However, he embraced intellectual rigor over violence. When driving to UC Riverside and exiting at University Avenue, drivers are greeted by an unexpectedly colorful mural painted on the underpass. Known as the Gluck Gateway Mural, it includes a depiction of the Costos. In the mural, they stand under a painted arch, with children sitting at their feet examining Indian basketry. The prominent location of this mural welcoming all visitors to campus serves as a reminder of the role of the Costos, who donated their personal papers and private collection to establish the Rupert Costo Library of the American Indian at the Tomás Rivera Library. The Society recognized that without information and knowledge, it would be difficult for non-Indians to empathize with Indian priorities.

By the early 1980s, the Costos remained committed to continuing their important work, but began to slow down due to their advancing ages. Regularly scheduled publications disappeared, and the organization diminished and ceased operating with Costo's failing health. Its formal dissolution occurred in 1986, though the Indian Historian Press briefly continued to function in a limited way.

More than fifty years have passed since the formal incorporation of the Society, and many founding members may be gone, but the dialogue and activities sparked by their direct actions can be observed throughout California and Indian Country. The activism of the AIHS demonstrated California Indians were not passive. The organization spoke out against anything it considered destructive to Indians. In all of its activities, the society remained committed to education and tribal self-determination. The legacy of the organization may be observed throughout California in the everyday activism: the continued fight for self-determination, Indian parents ensuring their children are treated equally in public schools, Indian students graduating, publications dedicated to Indians, and Indians insisting their voices are heard.

CULTURE AND
LANGUAGE

MARIA EVANGELISTE

GREG SARRIS

Her name was Maria, which was what the priest at St. Rose Church called all of the Indian girls, even this girl, Maria Evangeliste, who ironed his vestments and each Sunday played the violin so beautifully as the communicants marched to the altar to receive the sacraments that Jesus was said to smile down from the rafters at the dispensation of his body and blood.

That was why on a Friday, when she hadn't returned by nightfall, and by Sunday Mass, when there was still no sign of her, the priest worried as much as her family did, and after Mass notified the sheriff. The flatbed wagon that she had been driving was found by an apple farmer outside his stable, as if the old, pale-gray gelding was waiting to be unhitched and led to a stall inside. The two cherrywood chairs she'd purchased on the priest's behalf stood upright, still on the wagon bed, wedged between bales of straw. The priest had contracted the chairs for his rectory from a carpenter in Bodega; and Maria, needing any small amount of compensation, offered to drive the old gelding a nearly ten-mile trip west and then back. Still, she should have returned before nightfall, for she had left at dawn, the priest's money for the carpenter secure in her coat pocket.

A number of things could've happened to her. The horse might've spooked, jerking the wagon such that if she wasn't paying close attention she would've been tossed to the ground. She might be lying on the roadside someplace, knocked unconscious, a broken back, God forbid a broken neck. She could've been raped, left in the brush somewhere, even. At the time, in 1903, American Indians had not yet been granted US citizenship and therefore had no recourse in a US court. A lone Coast Miwok girl in Sonoma County was easy prey for marauding American men and boys who roamed the back roads, as the old Indians used to say, like packs of dogs.

But wouldn't they have hesitated, considering the possibility that Maria Evangeliste was a US citizen of Mexican descent, a guise many Indians used? Surely, approaching the wagon they would have seen the wooden cross hanging from her neck. If that didn't stop them, she had the ultimate defense, an embroidered crimson sash the priest wore at mass, which he had given her that morning as proof of protection from the Church, and which she'd kept folded in her other pocket, ready in the event someone should assault her, even if only to search her pockets to steal the priest's money for the carpenter. But none of these things happened.

As she rounded a hilly curve on the dirt road, which is now paved and called Occidental Road, she spotted two women. They were Indian women in long nineteenth-century dresses, scarves covering their heads and tied under their chins, and Maria Evangeliste recognized them immediately. They were twin sisters, childless elderly Southern Pomo women from the outskirts of Sebastopol, just a couple miles up the road. They did not resemble one another, one twin short and stout, the other taller, much darker, the color of oak bark. But, at that moment, hardly would Maria Evangeliste have remarked at their appearance, or the fact that, side by side, they stood in the middle of the road halting her passage, or even that she was in the vicinity of the rumored secret cave old people talked about in revered whispers. She understood what was happening without thinking, knew all at once. So when the taller of the two women commanded her off the wagon with only a nod of the chin, she knew she had no choice but to get down and follow them. And, it is told, that was how it started, how the twin sisters took Maria Evangeliste to train her as a Human Bear.

———

Why Maria Evangeliste was traveling on Occidental Road is a mystery. The usual route from Santa Rosa to the coastal town of Bodega was, and still is, the road west across the lagoon to the town of Sebastopol and then more or less straight to the coast. Returning from Bodega, she would have had to venture north along one of two or three narrow roads, wide paths really, to reach what is now Occidental Road—which would have been a longer, circuitous way to go, not to mention more dangerous given that she would be more isolated in the event she was assaulted. There was also greater risk of the old horse stumbling, some kind of accident with the wagon, on an unreliable road. Did she not want to pass through the town of Sebastopol because it was Friday, late in the day, and gangs of men off work from the sawmill and nearby orchards would already be gathered around the pubs, men who were drinking and might catch sight of her alone? There was an encampment of Indians where Occidental Road emptied onto the Santa Rosa plain—had she a friend she wanted to visit? Winter rain flooded, and still floods, the lagoon—was she traveling at a time when the water was high, when she needed to cross the northern bridge over the lagoon rather than the bridge in Sebastopol?

Following an ancient story of how the Human Bear cult started, in which a lone boy picking blackberries was kidnapped by grizzly bears and afforded their secrets and indomitable physical prowess, it is said that most initiates to the cult were likewise kidnapped. Human Bears might watch a young person carefully for some time, months or even years, regarding the young person's suitability for induction.

Stories are told of Human Bears traveling far distances to study a potential initiate, often in the guise of wanting only to see an old friend or to trade. They might even warn chosen individuals of their impending abduction, reminding them that they had no choice henceforth but to acquiesce and keep silent. Had Maria Evangeliste made arrangements beforehand, perhaps driven the priest's wagon north to fulfill her obligation?

Four days later, on a Tuesday morning, she returned to the clapboard house west of town where she lived with her family and a changing assembly of relatives forever in search of work. The small house, said to be owned by a dairy rancher for whom her father worked, sat above Santa Rosa Creek. Behind the house, lining the creek, was a stand of willow trees. A relative of my grandmother's, who first told me this story, said Maria Evangeliste appeared from behind the trees. Another older relative once pointed to a bald hillside while we were driving on Occidental Road and mentioned the story, claiming that Maria Evangeliste was first discovered standing in front of her house, not coming from behind the willows, and that in the faint morning light she was still as stone. Both versions posit that she was unharmed, returned as she had left, groomed, unsullied.

She could not tell where she had been. Did she lie, perhaps say that she lost control of the wagon after the horse spooked? Did she say as much in order to lead others to believe she'd run off with a young man? What was the sheriff told? The priest? However the case was resolved in the minds of the sheriff and the priest—whether from whatever story the girl might've relayed or from whatever either of them surmised themselves about what happened—the Indians were not so easily satisfied. For the Indians—or at least enough of them to pass on a story, anyway—the girl's answers were suspect and pointed to only one possible outcome: the two old twins in Sebastopol had found a successor.

——

I visited the bald hillside, parked my car on Occidental Road, then crawled under a barbed wire fence and hiked through brush and looming redwood trees, dark shade. Where would the secret cave be—this side of the hill, below the steep face of naked rock, or around the backside? Would such a cave exist still? Might not loggers or farmers have destroyed it long ago? Unable to see past a thicket of blackberry bramble, I could no longer look back and see the road. The outcropping of rock, exposed above the curtain of treetops, was a face with crater formations and crevices, as if the hill, like an enormous and uninhibited animal, was observing my approach. I became agitated. The story filled me. Oh, these are modern times, I told myself. What's a story these days? If anything, I should be worrying about trespassing on private property. Nonetheless, I stopped. Looking over the blackberry bramble to the trees, I attempted to regain my bearings, again trying to gauge my distance from the road.

In 1903, when the twin sisters abducted Maria Evangeliste, loggers had leveled the trees a second time—or were about to. The magnificent original redwoods, reaching down from the Oregon border to present-day Monterey County, were for the most part cleared between 1830 and 1870. The trees before me, a third growth of redwoods, were about a hundred years old, and a hundred feet tall. In 1903 the gigantic original trees that once sheltered the grizzly bears were gone; and, whether or not the second stand of trees still stood, the grizzly was extinct in the region, killed decades before by Mexican vaqueros and American settlers. The Human Bear cult, like the grizzly bear, was dependent on the trees and on open landscape unencumbered by fences and ranchers protective of livestock. Stories abound—even among local non-Indians—of ranchers felling a bear only to find when they went to retrieve the carcass an empty hide. The twin sisters, how did they instruct their last recruit? Did they show Maria Evangeliste a route that was still safe to travel under a moonless nighttime sky? Did they have only memories to offer, power songs unsung outside the old cave?

Secret societies, such as the Human Bear cult, both perpetuated and reflected Pomo and Coast Miwok worldviews, in which every human, just as every aspect of the landscape, possessed special—and secret—powers. Cult members with their special power and connection to the living world played an integral role in the well-being of the village. Human Bears, assuming the grizzly's strength and extraordinary sense of smell, could locate and retrieve food from far distances. They also possessed "protection," which sometimes consisted of knowledge of a feature of the landscape they might use, such as a cave, but which often was in the form of songs that could cause illness, sometimes death, to anyone who might attempt to harm them. The mere existence of Human Bears would thus make you think twice about harming anyone. Same with a bird, a tree, any tiny stone. Respect becomes the only guarantee of survival. This respect is predicated on remembering that, even with unique power, you are not alone, absolute. As Mabel McKay told me, "Be careful when someone [or something] catches your attention. You don't know what spirit it is. Be thoughtful." The Kashaya Pomo elders refer to Europeans as *pala-cha*, miracles: instead of being punished for killing people and animals, chopping down trees, damming and dredging the waterways, the Europeans just kept coming.

There were numerous secret cults. Many were associated with animals—bobcats, grizzly bears, even birds and snakes. Others were associated with a particular place—a meadow, a canyon, an underwater cave where the spirit of the place empowered its respective cult members. Cults were often gender based: women's Bear cults were considered among the most powerful. In all cases, cult initiates endured long periods of training, not only learning about, for instance, the essentials of their animal powers but simultaneously about the larger environment as well.

Sonoma County, about an hour north of San Francisco, was at the time of European contact one of the most geographically complex and biologically diverse places on earth. Below arid hills, covered with only bunchgrass and the occasional copse of oak and bay laurel, were rich wetlands, inland bays, lakes, a meandering lagoon, and a substantial river and numerous creeks where hundreds of species of waterfowl flew up so thick as to obliterate the sun for hours at a time. Immense herds of elk, pronghorn, and blacktail deer grazed along these waterways on any number of clovers and sedges. West, lining the coastal hills, were redwoods so thick that several yards into a forest all was dark as night. The shifting shoreline, steep cliffs dropping to the water or to broad sandy beaches, was rich too, rife with edible sea kelps and dozens of species of clams, mussels, abalone, and fish—salmon the most prized. Despite these distinct environments—arid hills, lush plains and wetlands, redwood forests—the landscape was usually inconsistent, tricky even. Amidst the arid hills below Sonoma Mountain were numerous lakes and spring-fed marshes.

Meadows, prairie-like, appeared unexpectedly in the otherwise dense and dark redwood forests. A narrow creek might empty into a wide and deep perch-filled pond just on the other side of a small, barren-looking knoll. Traveling through an expanse of marshy plain you might discover, stepping from waist-high sedges, a carpet of rock a mile wide and several miles long, habitat for snakes and lizards that would otherwise be found in the drier foothills. Nothing appeared quite what it seemed. The landscape, complex in design and texture, demanded reflection, study. The culture that grew out of a ten-thousand-year relationship with the place became like it, not just in thought but in deed. Pomo and Coast Miwok art—the most complicated and intricate basketry found among Indigenous people anywhere—tells the story.

Human Bears learned the details of the landscape: where a fish-ripe lake hid behind a bend, where a thicket of blackberries loaded with fruit sat tucked below a hillside. At the same time, regardless of their unique ability to travel great distances and seek out food sources for the village, they could not disrespect the hidden lake or thicket of berries, needing always to know the requirements for taking the fish or fruit. The lake had a special—and potentially dangerous—spirit, just as the Human Bear, and so too the blackberry thicket. Developing a heightened sense of the Human Bear's unique power necessitated a heightened sense of the land. Ultimately, the Human Bear cult didn't play an integral role only in the well-being of the village but also, more precisely, in the well-being of the village within the larger world.

By 1903 most of the landscape was transformed. Gone were the vast wetlands. The water table throughout the region had dropped an average of two hundred feet. Creeks went dry in summer. The big trees were gone. Many of the great animals were extinct in the region, not just the grizzly bears but the herds of elk and pronghorn, and the mighty condors gliding the thermals with their fourteen-foot wingspans. Regarding these remarkable ancestral birds, Tsupu, my great-great-great-grandmother, sitting atop a wagon toward the end of the nineteenth century, gazed up at the empty sky and asked, "How are the people going to dance without feathers?" If there was a route safe for Maria Evangeliste to travel as a Human Bear in 1903, would there still exist a familiar bountiful blackberry thicket? An ocean cove where she might collect a hundred pounds of clams?

Just as the landscape was transformed, increasingly so too was the eons-old way of thinking about it. Catholic missionaries put in the minds of Coast Miwok and Pomo villagers the notion of an eternal and spiritual life that was elsewhere, that could not be derived and experienced from the land. The God of an elsewhere kingdom overruled, in fact deemed as evil, anything on the earth that might be considered equally powerful, worthy of reverence and awe. While Christianity was forced upon the Natives, usually under conditions of duress and enslavement, the new religion might have made sense. After European contact, Coast Miwok and Pomo no doubt looked upon the transformed landscape and found that they recognized the place less and less, that, in essence, they were no longer home. Indeed miraculous, the new people could kill animals or level a hill without retribution. Couldn't their one almighty God from another world stop a Human Bear? Yes—seen once as necessary to life and land, a protector of the village, the Human Bear—or anyone who would participate in such things—was now more and more an enemy of our well-being, dangerous at best, possibly evil.

Did Maria Evangeliste know what stories people told about her? If, secretly, she left a cache of ripe fruit or clams outside her home as Human Bears once did in the villages, might she not implicate herself, reveal her secret life, in a world hostile to that life? Wouldn't relatives deem the food the devil's work and toss it out? She was the last Human Bear, they say. When did she stop visiting the cave? When was it over?

The morning she returned she said that she had lost control of the wagon. Or she said she visited a friend and hadn't tied the old gelding well enough. Or she said she met a man. In any event, she went that afternoon with the priest and retrieved the wagon with its still-upright rectory chairs from the apple farmer. And that was how, before sunset, she came back to town, driving the wagon as if nothing was unusual, as if four days had not passed at all. She continued to play violin in the church. She was still entrusted with work for the priest. Sometime later she married a Mexican immigrant. They had eleven children, all of whom lived to adulthood. A great-granddaughter sat next to me in catechism class. The last time I saw her, Maria Evangeliste, that is, was sometime in the early 1970s, about ten years before she died at the age of ninety. I was at a funeral in St. Rose Church. She was in the crowd of mourners, a small Indian woman in a dark dress. She wore a veil, respectfully.

———

I left town around then and did not return for thirty years. I visited, seeing family, and I came back for tribal business. But I wasn't really back—I wasn't home—which I hadn't yet realized, and didn't understand until later. I wrote about Sonoma County—stories, essays, plays—from memory. In fact, I'd hardly written about anyplace else. But what was I remembering? What did I understand?

Sonoma County had changed dramatically. From the center of what once was small-town Santa Rosa, strip malls and housing developments spread over the vast plain, covering irrigated clover and vetch pastures, fruit orchards and strawberry fields. Gone, the black-and-white-spotted Holstein cows. Gone, rows of prune and pear trees; the apple orchards north and east of Sebastopol, almost each and every one was routed by grapes: pinot noir, cabernet. The arid foothills are now also covered in grapes—gone, the copses of oak and bay laurel there. Visiting, I noticed these changes; coming home for good, I saw how thorough they were, how far-reaching. Where was my home?

I bought the house on Sonoma Mountain. Bay laurel trees, live oaks, and white oaks surround the house; and, past the trees, there is an expansive view west over vineyard-covered hills and the urban sprawl below, to the Pacific Ocean, which is where at night the web of streetlights stops—and where on a very clear night the full moon lights the sea. That light—that path of moon on the water—was how the dead found their way to the next world, or so our ancestors said. And those same ancestors gathered peppernuts from the six-hundred-year-old bay tree outside my gate. But I was like that—suspended between the old bay tree and the far horizon—as I negotiated what it meant to be home. I hadn't lived on the mountain before. I grew up below, in Santa Rosa.

Then the place remembered me. Stories beckoned. The dead rose, collected with the living, so that more and more the landscape became a meeting hall of raucous voices. I knew the faces. Not merely my tribal members, as if I was convening a tribal meeting, but the land itself—mountain and plain, oak trees and city lights, birds and animals, Indians and non-Indians, Mexicans, Italians, Blacks, Filipinos, Jews—whomever and whatever I'd known, whomever and whatever I knew, was before me, beckoning. Yes, the dead and the living—how could anything die this way? History, it's no less tangible, palpable, than that grandmother under whose care you found yourself. In a kitchen you have known all your life, with its familiar smells and colors, this grandmother sets a plate of warm tortillas on the table with a bowl of chicken soup and says, "Eat."

Driving here and there, to the university, to the laundromat, the market, here and there with no worry of catching an airplane, seeing this relative or that friend before I left again, I had time, the idleness that accompanies routine, and the old lady with the tortillas and soup was able to catch my attention. Driving over Wohler Bridge west of town—west of Santa Rosa—I glance down and see the riverbank and willows: a bonfire lights a moonless night and Filipino men are gathered around the fire there, and my grandmother, a seventeen-year-old Coast Miwok girl, eyes my grandfather for the first time, a *pinoy* dandy in his pin-striped suit, the big gold watch chain dangling from his breast pocket reflecting firelight, and the blood-letting fighting cocks clashing midair, their tiny silhouettes jumping in his watch glass like a pair of enchanted dancers performing a wild tango my grandmother already wants to learn. From behind the townhouses on Coffey Lane, Holstein cows emerge one by one, full udders swaying, and collect in front of the 7-Eleven where Mrs. Andreoli, forty and soon to be a widow, opens the wooden gate to her milk barn. And Old Uncle, old Pomo medicine man—"don't say his real name"—he's on a bench uptown in Courthouse Square, suspenders and fedora, or he's in his garden behind the fairgrounds, where two hours ago he built a fire below the tall cornstalks and thick gourd vines. Witness as he holds now an ember in the palm of his hand and sees and hears in the orange-red ash "all manner of things": people and animals, songs, old earth rules. Isn't this how some folks saw Maria Evangeliste when she returned on foot after four days to her parents' house?

Years later, when they found themselves next to her, scooping rice in the market or picking prunes in the heat-dusty orchards, didn't they still think and remember?

Here I am not a stranger. Looking back, I see how I'd been a stranger, a newcomer at best, wherever else I had lived. I drove back and forth to the university, to the market, in Los Angeles. I did errands in Manhattan. But it wasn't the same. No stories. No old earth rules. Or, put it this way, I had to learn the stories, listen to the rules as a newcomer, and, like that, as mindful as I could be, make a home. Still, Fifth Avenue midday remained less busy for me than a remote redwood grove in Sonoma County. I could be alone in Yellowstone. Or the Grand Canyon. These latter places in particular, beautiful, yes. And solitude. But then what is solitude, however blissful? Can it be experienced except by disengagement from the land's stories, its spirits? Wilderness. The old people said the land became wild after we became separated from it, when there were no longer enough of us to hear its demands and tend to it accordingly. Could Thoreau and Muir experience the landscape as pristine, and know solitude in it as such, if they knew its stories? If that old woman was there, tortillas and chicken soup at hand, would the land be silent?

———

At a tribal General Council meeting, I saw Maria Evangeliste's great-granddaughter, the same girl I knew from catechism class. Now approaching sixty, a heavyset woman with a shock of dyed black hair, she sat amidst the sea of faces listening to questions and answers regarding the status of our casino. She looked disgruntled, arms crossed over her chest, face puckered in a scowl, and walked out before the meeting was over, leaving me wondering if she was mad at me or someone else on the council or just at life in general.

Her life, from what I'd heard, hadn't been easy. Five children. Two were in prison. One was dead. Ten grandchildren, five of whom she was raising. Where was the soft-faced, flat-limbed teenager who'd listened with me as Sister Agnes Claire attempted to explain the Holy Ghost?

Some tribal members say I was away too long, that I'd gotten "too white." Did she feel that way about me, that I didn't know my people well enough any longer? Her husband, the father of her five children, was a Mexican immigrant. Did she know that her great-grandfather was a Mexican immigrant also? Had she heard the stories about Maria Evangeliste? Did she care?

Perhaps I write for no other reason than to leave a record for her or anyone besides me who might care, a set of tracks, however faint, down the mountain into the plain and back, connecting to those infinite other pathways that take us and keep us in the land and its life here. But this is what I'm thinking now, as I consider what it means to be a writer here. It wasn't what I was thinking during the meeting seeing Maria Evangeliste's great-granddaughter.

———

I went to the cave. Driving on Occidental Road, I was quite certain of the spot my cousin had pointed to years before—the bald hillside—if for no other reason than that a hippie commune was there at the time, a settlement of teepees past the redwoods, which I mentioned, prompting from my cousin her story of Maria Evangeliste.

The road curved under a canopy of oak trees and tall pines; four o'clock in the afternoon, autumn, the land was already in shadow, the road lead-gray like the occasional patch of sky above. Human

Bears traveled only at night in the pitch black; they did not set out in human form for their caves until late at night either. Secrecy was the initiate's first rule. Mabel McKay once told me of a father up in Lake County who, curious about his daughter's whereabouts at night, unwittingly followed her to a Human Bear cave, whereupon her cult sisters gruesomely murdered him right before her eyes. "Ain't supposed to be seeing them things," Mabel said. "Respect." With this story in mind and the landscape darkening around me, it's no wonder that, past the barbed wire fence and into the trees, I was agitated, so much so that when I looked back and couldn't see the road, I stopped. Respect? Was I disrespecting? These are modern times, I kept telling myself. What's a story these days? Wasn't I curious just to see the cave as a landmark, an outpost of memory? Yes, nothing more. I would leave something, a dollar bill, my handkerchief, out of respect. A lone jay shrieked from somewhere on the other side of the blackberry bramble. I looked up, above the line of trees, to the outcropping of rock, enormous and still watchful, then I left.

It was enough, I told myself. Enough. But I kept thinking of Maria Evangeliste. In the car, driving back to town, my excitement only grew. Past the overreaching branches and thick brush on either side of the road, I saw how a uniform gray light enveloped the land, a color such that everything I could see seemed made from it. I had never seen the light in such a way at that time of day; and, I thought that though Maria Evangeliste, after her first four nights with the twin sisters, emerged and came back to town at dawn, the light and land must have looked this way, new, as she had never seen it before. Then I rounded a curve and, coming down the hill, I saw the broad plain clear to the mountain. City lights shone like tiny flags in the gathering darkness. I pulled over, stopped the car. No, I thought then. After Maria Evangeliste first came out of the cave, it was like this: stories, places—an entire land—that she knew day or night, light or no light, not as if for the first time, but better.

LEARNING HOW TO FISH: A LANGUAGE HOMECOMING JOURNAL

DEBORAH A. MIRANDA

And he saith unto them, Follow me, and I will make you fishers of men. And they straightway left their nets, and followed him.
—*Matthew 4:19–20*

Monday

8 a.m.: coffee

9 a.m.: blessing

10 a.m.: welcome. "Give a person a fish, and she'll eat for the day," Leanne tells us, "but teach her to fish and she'll feed herself and her family forever." I sit in a classroom at UC Berkeley and take notes. I can't believe I'm here. Can't believe I've done this to myself again: an intensive summer language program. Didn't I go crazy enough the first time around, with Spanish? Teach me to fish. Yeah, right.

The Franciscan missionaries assigned to Alta California loved their metaphors too. Father Serra wrote of California's Indigenous inhabitants that "before long, they will be caught in the apostolic and evangelical net," likening himself and his fellow priests to the Fishers of Men called upon by Christ to spread the Gospel. I've always been a bit bothered by this image, however; the comparison between catching fish and catching souls just never worked for me. After all—one *eats* what one catches; swallows, consumes, devours. One uses that flesh as fuel for one's own body. Catching Indian bodies and souls like catching fish? It makes me wonder about alternative, darker definitions of the word "save."

I'm not sure I can survive an entire week here, submersed in California Indian languages. It all started with a phone call and my sister Louise gushing, "This is incredible," in a voice happier than I had ever heard her use before. "I'm learning new words every hour, I seem to understand them even before David explains what they mean, I wrote a prayer, we study all day and all night . . . I never thought this could happen, but our language is out there, *we can learn it!*"

It was as if someone had given her a brand new pole and a big box of tackle and said, "Come on in, which hook do you want to try first?" My sister had become a Fisher of Words.

So here we sit, two years later, at the Breath of Life conference, a biannual event sponsored by UC Berkeley's linguistics department, in partnership with the nonprofit group Advocates for Indigenous California Language Survival. I'd encouraged Louise to apply that first year. After all, she lived in California. (I was way out in Virginia.) After all, she was involved with the tribal council and meetings. (I was just a poet, an academic, dealing with theories about indigeneity.) After all, learning Esselen or Chumash is about a billion light-years beyond me (a woman who almost had a nervous breakdown trying to survive three years of Spanish for her Ph.D. requirements). I had a lot of excuses, and eventually Louise countered every single one.

But secretly, I know my monolingual brain is completely occupied by English; I can't imagine taking decolonization to those deep dark places where Indigenous languages hide. I just hope I don't embarrass my sister.

Let me explain right here that my sister Louise is brilliant. Two years after her first Breath of Life conference, she has compiled the first Esselen-English dictionary, coauthoring it with her mentor, David Shaul. Louise accomplished this not with an academic degree, not with government funding, not with a fellowship or grant, and not with any technical support or materials other than her home computer. She accomplished this mammoth task while sitting in her living room in San Jose, sifting through research papers and copies of field notes, and with several short visits from her mentor, who was usually away working on an entirely different project. She accomplished this while running for chair of the Ohlone/Costanoan-Esselen Nation, caring for a granddaughter, husband, and elderly mother, and managing a household, both before and after knee replacement surgery!

God, I hope there's not ten different tenses.

———

Tuesday

8 a.m.: coffee

9 a.m.: blessing

9:30 a.m.: homework

Oh faithful band of linguists and students who volunteer their time, expertise, and encouragement! Do you really want us to read a passage in our language out loud on the second day? I stumble over *Tanoch kalul hikpa*, "The woman sees the fish." Subject, object, verb. I thrash my way through *Iniki tanoch mashaipa*, "This woman is hungry." Demonstratives—the equivalents of the English words "this" and "that." (What is Louise doing over there? Jesus! She's writing a freaking book!) Leanne, her cheerful face bobbing from one table of fricatives and glottal stops to another, reminds us that Breath of Life does not—cannot—teach California Indians our tribal languages in one week. "What Breath of Life *tries* to do is present hungry people with the tools and materials you need to learn how to fish for yourselves."

So Leanne and her magnificent crew of volunteer linguists, students, and museum/archive/library staff give us a crash course in how to do research on California Indian languages, with specific focus on our individual languages and the materials close at hand in California, especially at UC Berkeley. UC Berkeley, according to Leanne, has the largest collections of California Indian language and cultural materials in the world. I call them "how-to tours." Every afternoon, we visit a major collection and the tour always includes not just a general introduction to the materials, but hands-on instructions for using those materials to research a specific tribal language and/or culture. The Phoebe Hearst Museum of Anthropology. Survey of California and Other Indian Languages. An archival information site at Doe Library. The Berkeley Language Center. The Bancroft Library's extensive collection of microfilms. If my brain doesn't shrivel up first, my feet will.

Today we received special permission to view the baskets in Basket Storage. Going into the facility was like visiting our relatives in jail: sweet, bittersweet. We left purses, backpacks, food and drink outside. We donned plastic gloves. We entered a huge room full of white towers, inside of which are set deep drawers and shelving, covered with—oh, filled with—baskets made by the hands of our ancestors. Gina found one made by her grandmother. She cried. We could touch them (with gloves on), photograph them, talk to them, pray over them, sing to them. We were allowed to bring in rattles and clappers. The shaking seeds like rain, elderberry claps like thunder, and voices of our little Breath of Life tribe were springs of life in the quiet climate-controlled room. It was a heartbreaking visit. We could not take them home.

—

Wednesday

8 a.m.: coffee

9 a.m.: blessing

9:30 a.m.: homework

10:00 a.m.: class

Every fishing hole has its quirks, little tricks to finding the best fish, special hooks that work there but not over here, and secret techniques passed down only to a lucky few. I guess it's the same with trying to learn a California Indian language: some libraries have certain field notes; others don't. One linguist's field notes are on microfilm but only at one particular branch of one particular school; another linguist's research has been processed and published as articles, but in obscure journals. Some "field notes" are actually letters and journals kept by explorers, missionaries, or entrepreneurs, scattered all over the planet in various museums, collections, libraries. Some primary materials—the actual notes themselves—are found only at a tiny nondescript storage area you'd never suspect.

But the one guaranteed thing? It's never all in one place, it's never all perfectly clear, and it's never going to be easy. Put on your hip boots and wade right in. Today, I am up to my neck in the existential *cha'a*—as in "we exist!"

So I'm not surprised that Esselen has no real verb for "to be" or for "to have." You just *are*. It just *is*. Louise tries to teach me some sleight-of-hand linguistic maneuver to get around this, but I'm thick as a brick. *Kalul yakiski-k*—"the fish (is) large" and *mawipas saleki-k*—"the song (is) good." Somehow, the intention of "is" is communicated via this "k" sound stuck on to the end of the noun. My brain wrestles with constructing a sentence that, to my poor English-trained neural pathways, means "The fish large is." "That's it!" Louise crows, "That sounds good!"

"That sounds like Yoda," I mutter. But I'm pleased.

—

Thursday

8 a.m.: coffee

9 a.m.: blessing

9:30 a.m.: homework

10:00 a.m.: class

This year's Breath of Life class is over sixty participants, representing more than twenty-five different California Indian languages and major dialects of languages. It's one of the larger groups, Leanne says. That's a lot of Indian souls literally given the "breath of life" to take home to their communities and families.

We joke that for this week, we are all one tribe: the Breath of Life tribe, located in the Berkeley homeland. We move to our tribal rhythm: breakfast together in the seminar room, followed by sharing of our individual homework assignments and a lecture about linguistic analysis. At noon we break for lunch, then head off to various tours and little study groups scattered throughout dorms and the campus till dinnertime; in the evenings, more study groups (frequently led by our mentors and their assistants) go on late into the night. Instead of sitting around a communal fire grilling juicy salmon, we sit around dorm rooms or on outdoor benches grilling each other on vocabulary, conjugation, plurals, and the always-popular curse words.

Somewhere in the Harrington notes, Isabel Meadows remembers that Fulgencio Cantua told her, "very tasty, our language." I imagine our words being crispy or salty or smooth as a ripe fig. I like the idea that our language has flavor, texture, scent, yet can never be consumed. I tell Louise about Fulgencio's comment; she tells everyone else, and we end the evening with great smacking of lips and satisfied rubbing of tummies. "Oh, *that's* why they make those sounds, like they're savoring each syllable!" Anyone looking at us from the outside would run in the other direction.

—

Friday

8 a.m.: coffee

9 a.m.: blessing

9:30 a.m.: homework

10:00 a.m.: class

Louise and I call each other *Ichi* now—"sister."

Louise writes beautifully in Esselen, and her speaking voice/ pronunciation sounds rounded, natural. It reminds me of the way our dad used to slur his English so that the edges of the words came out softer than everyone else's. Maybe his Spanish did that too, but I never heard him speak enough of it to tell. I remember how our dad's dad, Grandpa Tom, spoke Indian in his last days, how his son, Uncle Tommy, was shocked to realize not just that this was an Indian language, but that he, too, understood it! How it came flooding back to him after six decades of dormancy: his mother tongue. We all knew that our grandmother Marquesa and her mother, Dolores, spoke Chumash together; Louise remembers playing under the kitchen table and hearing them chatter as they worked. But it never occurred to any of us that Dad and his younger brothers might have soaked up enough of that language to make any difference. As the oldest, Uncle Tommy must have heard the most, before the conversations stopped when our great-grandmother died—he was probably the only one to retain anything at all. Later, Tommy told us, he went down to Santa Ynez and spoke with some of the old folks there. *They understood what he was saying.* So was Grandpa Tom speaking his wife's language? Or was Esselen enough like Samala (Santa Ynez Chumash) to bridge the gap? Or had the family developed a kind of hybrid dialect of the two? It's one of those California Indian mysteries. And it makes me wonder if this kind of tenuous connection—literally listening under the table—is what gives Louise such fluency, as if she is coming home to a language at last, rather than learning it for the first time.

If she is coming home to the language, the language is coming home to her, too. *Lex welel*—our language—must have been lonely all this time.

———

Saturday

9 a.m.: blessing

10 a.m.: participant projects

Louise gave the blessing this morning—in Esselen.

I read my first poem in Esselen, sweated out onto the page with much help from David, our mentor, and Ruth, his assistant; pushed off my awkward tongue by Louise's determined coaching.

Did I say we were hungry Indians? We are starving! Starving for our languages.

At this morning's presentation of individual projects, I heard California Indians use their languages to speak prayers, sing songs, create original poems and stories, retell oral histories, croon lullabies to their babies, make jokes, invent picture books, caption family scrapbooks— Clara even reveled in finding a phrase that means something like "piece of shit!"

Listening, watching, I realized that virtually every aspect of culture was presented: religion, music, oral and written literatures, linguistic play . . . don't try telling a Breath of Life participant that our cultures are dead. We have become Fishers of Words, but we practice a catch and release system: snag those little silver gems, then release them back out into the wider world as quickly and lovingly as possible. Let them go forth and multiply. Whatever allegory you want to use, the work of language recovery and renewal takes patience, near-obsessive persistence, and the generosity of many.

We understand now: you just gotta know the right place to drop that line.

FALSE IMAGES AND YOUNG MINDS: SOUNDING OFF ON HISTORY, RACISM, AND EDUCATION

JAYDEN LIM

The lake was painted red with the blood of her family. She looked up to see the sun peering through the rippling water. She could see the black boots that belonged to the US Calvary stomping through the water and breaking the silence. She shook underwater with the fear of discovery. What if they find her? Will they kill her? She held the tule tight between her two chapped lips. This plant was the only chance at survival. She took deep breaths through the straw-like plant. She tried to calm herself, but it was impossible. Calmness and slaughter don't quite go together. This was the 1850 Bloody Island Massacre she was experiencing. She was among the very few child survivors.

In the fall of 1847, Andrew Kelsey and Charles Stone bought Salvador Vallejo's cattle operation. Vallejo had trained the local Pomo Natives as vaqueros (Indian cowboys), but Stone and Kelsey's treatment of the Native community in Big Valley was extremely brutal. Natives were outraged in the fall of 1849 when, in the grip of gold fever, Kelsey forced fifty to one hundred Native men to accompany him to the gold fields. Only two returned alive. Stone and Kelsey became more careless and brutal after that. Shootings and beatings took place regularly. Women and children were raped and enslaved. When Chief Augustine's wife became the subject of attention, he organized an attack. His wife poured water onto the powder charges of Kelsey and Stone's firearms, and Natives burst into the house at dawn. Kelsey was killed, but Stone had leaped through a window as an act of desperation. Stone's body was later found; he had been brained by a rock.

In the spring of 1850, the US Calvary came to "punish" the Natives for their "misbehavior." Two hundred Pomo people were slaughtered. During the attack, one of my ancestors, Napo, had told her children to hide in the lake and breathe through the tule. They ran to the lake while Napo tried to find another way to escape. Napo's children survived the Bloody Island Massacre. Many of the children lived to adulthood. Elizabeth Posh, a grandchild of one of the survivors, gave birth to nine children. Only six of them lived to adulthood, one of which was my great-grandmother, Matilda Myers. She had a child at fifteen years old and named him Joe Myers.

Joe has spent his life fighting against the injustices, violence, and poverty he experienced living on the Pinoleville reservation near Ukiah. He educates non-Natives who need to better understand the misconceptions and stereotypes that Natives face. Native people suffer from stereotypes in addition to the external traumas that shapes their lives. The instinct for survival has guided our people through generations of painful experiences. Though the pages of our history are sad, the ability of our ancestors to overcome these challenges and save our culture gives us strength and purpose. From my ancestors I have inherited the ability to survive, adapt, dream, excel, and beat the odds at all costs. I am not a princess, animal, savage, drunk, stupid, or extinct.

Before fourth grade, most children think that Native American women are princesses and the men are buff killing machines. Thanks to Disney's *Pocahontas*, even some children that are older than ten years of age still believe the misconceptions. They also believe that we have mystical powers and that we can't count beyond one hundred. This shows how Native Americans are classified as characters in a fairytale. These classifications oversimplify who we are and take attention away from more important issues. What's the truth about Native American women? According to the *New York Times*, "Native American women are also at a high risk of sexual and physical abuse, recorded at three and a half times higher than the national average. This estimate is very low because 70 percent of abuse cases go unreported, often due to mistrust Native American women feel toward government and police. Seventy percent of the violence experienced by Native American women is from non-Native American men."

The Hollywood Indian is the most common stereotype. Headdresses, moccasins, buckskin, and beads are common accessories. They enforce stereotypes because they are the most common representation of Native Americans offered to the public eye. These false images are engraved into young minds. These pictures appear on beer bottles, in movies and books, and as sports mascots. For example, the "Party Rock Anthem" shuffle is really a smoke dance. The smoke dance was originally a war dance only performed by men. People don't understand the value of these dances to Native people. These ceremonial practices represent our cultures and connect today's tribal ceremonies to the past.

The Hollywood Indian stereotype is for the movie obsessed, but there is another common stereotype among the knowledge obsessed, that Native Americans came across the land bridge called the Bering Strait. This is the typical hook or introduction for starting a lesson on Native Americans. This theory has so many inconsistencies. Where is the evidence that supports this theory? There is no evidence. Though there is evidence that it did not happen. The Natives supposedly came across the Bering Strait about fifteen thousand years prior to Columbus's arrival in 1492. If we are using science as our measuring stick, there are ruins that are over twenty thousand years old in America. The Bering Strait theory is also offensive because it goes against the religions of Native people, which state that we have always been here. The late Standing Rock Sioux scholar Vine Deloria Jr. has significantly challenged this theory and referred to it as "scientific language for I don't know, but it sounds good and no one will check." In his book *Red Earth, White Lies: American Indians and the Myth of Scientific Fact*, he wrote, "An examination of the Bering Strait doctrine suggests that such a journey would have been nearly impossible even if there had been hordes of Paleo-Indians trying to get across the hypothetical land bridge. It appears that not even animals or plants really crossed this mythical connection between Asia and North America. The Bering Strait exists and existed only in the minds of scientists."

Why is this theory presented as fact? Is it to promote the romantic notion that America is a country of immigrants? Why are other theories or cultural beliefs not presented? Are we avoiding a discussion of what happened to aboriginal peoples? I understand that it may protect children from the reality of what occurred and will prevent questioning, but does it really help them in the long run? Preparing our youth for the future is what childhood is supposed to do. Writer Rebecca Stead says everyone is born with a veil. This veil is like a bride's veil and is somewhat see-through. It causes the world to look blurry, but we like it that way. Sometimes the wind lifts the veil so we can see the world for what it truly is. We can see glimpses of the good and the bad in the world. We need to lift the veil that our children wear so they can see the world for what it truly is.

There are many essential understandings that one must possess to teach accurately and sensitively about Native Americans. The most important one is for educators to realize Native Americans are all very diverse. Hundreds of tribes have thousands of different languages, ceremonies, songs, religions, etc. People sometimes come up to me and ask, "Can you speak Indian?" There are over six hundred tribes and even more languages, so of course I cannot speak "Indian." We need to address these issues as soon as possible. We need to protect children of Native American descent as well as others of all races from negative and inaccurate information. We can end the ripple effect of the traumas experienced by their ancestors.

Physical abuse has become very popular among all teenagers, and particularly in Native American students. We need to show them that things can and will get better. We can give you alternative lesson plans and resources, but you need to use them and take interest in them. Native youth have the right to know the truth. We need to work on decreasing the number of gasps in the room when an audience hears that Native women were raped by priests and soldiers. This is not merely Native history, it is American history and should be common knowledge. We need to communicate a factual history even if it is not complimentary to those who wrote it. Communication will help us address the issues together. As Agnes Repplier says, "Action may not always bring happiness, but there is no happiness without action."

WEAVING THROUGH THE COLLEGE EXPERIENCE

RIVER GARZA

I have never really thought about my college experience until now. Reflecting on it, I find it hard to narrow down the past three years of my life at the university into a representation that accurately expresses the growth, changes, and awakening I've gone through as a young Indigenous man in college.

As cliché as it sounds, college has been an interesting journey thus far, to say the least. I like to view and express my journey through college as being similar to that of someone learning how to weave a basket for the first time. Many Indigenous folks like myself are familiar with the process of basketweaving, but for those who aren't, it's a painstaking process that requires time, patience, and commitment. Just by looking at a basket one can sense the underlying complexity, respect the passion of a basketweaver, and feel the sense of tradition in this working piece of art.

For myself, I find it hard to see a basket and not wonder how many countless hours were spent weaving in and out, up and over, with a tenacity and sense of commitment that only the beauty of the final product can speak to. One can begin the process of learning how to weave by simply looking at a basket, knowing absolutely nothing about creating it yet desiring to make one. College had also been an abstract goal made possible and attainable by getting past the necessary hurdles.

I began my college journey like the rookie weaver who doesn't have even the slightest clue of where to start or how to go about creating something so magnificent. My journey into higher education began with me as an eager English major with pre-law aspirations, ready to change the world and set on making a difference in the future for the less fortunate. From the very beginning I embraced my journey into this semi-foreign land (although Pomona is only less than fifty miles away from my native Gardena). My first quarter of school was, as I'm sure it is for many freshmen, shocking! The college experience was in no way what I had expected it to be; I had never been exposed to so many different types of ideas and people in one confined place. It truly is a place of self-discovery. I was so bold and naive as to pledge a fraternity at one point, but soon after figured out it was not by any means meant for or accurate in representing me. As the school year progressed, I took a slew of different classes and eventually grew disillusioned with majoring in English and the concept of justice within the confines of our legal system. I eventually changed my major to economics, which at the time seemed like the logical choice, but I would decide later on that it was not for me.

During my first year of school, my most notable and favorite class was an intro Native American studies course taught by Dr. Sandy Kewanhaptewa-Dixon (Hopi). Her class served as my first exposure to Native faculty and contemporary Indigenous issues on a broader spectrum. I eventually became acquainted with Dr. Dixon and grew to love the class more and more, not only for the insight it provided within the scope of my own life but also because it exposed me to how other people interpret Indigenous peoples and our issues. Little did I know how much this one class would affect the course of my life.

The school year came and went, and one day during the early weeks of summer vacation I got a surprise email from Professor Dixon asking me if I wanted to be a mentor for a week-long summer pipeline program for Native high school students in its second year. She was coordinating it with Irvin Harrison (Navajo) at the Native American Student Center. It was a sign—an opportunity had presented itself for me to give back at a grassroots level to my community, potentially become a positive role model, and aid others during a time that had been confusing for me. I readily agreed to help with the program and began a relationship with Professor Dixon and the Native American Student Center that would eventually take me to new places like Alaska and introduce me to a multitude of people in the Southern California Native community who would become integral to my life. My teachers had arrived, those who would guide me in weaving this contemporary yet traditional beauty. The fibers and structure of my basket were starting to form. The foundation from which I would commence my weaving was becoming stronger; my traditional masterpiece was underway.

My second year of schooling wasn't much different from my first, except this time around I was renting an apartment off campus with some friends, progressing through my economics courses, and finally feeling comfortable going into the Native American Student Center and contributing to our campus community. The year was filled with procrastination, essays, group work, and a longing for summer vacation that nothing could seem to hinder. As the school year was coming to an end I was excited to say yes when Dr. Dixon asked me to join her and the rest of the pipeline staff for a second time. This time I would be head mentor for the young men and have more responsibilities. That year's pipeline went smoothly and I was more than excited to see familiar faces and hear their stories about progressing in high school and getting closer to college. I also relished the opportunity to meet new participants and help them any way I could. It's so exciting to see engaged Indigenous youth care about their college education and gain firsthand exposure to college before even enrolling as a student. I feel no greater sense of gratitude than seeing families take advantage of the programs universities offer and make college seem like more of an option. It was during this year, through Dr. Dixon, that I had the opportunity to work with students applying to college at Sherman Indian High School in Riverside.

The highlight of my second year was my Native American Contemporary Issues class. I took this course with an adjunct faculty who was teaching the class for Dr. Dixon for that quarter. If I can pinpoint why I enjoyed this course so much I think it was because it made me feel empowered, in the sense that I gained a broader understanding of the vast array of complex issues that we face as Indigenous peoples. I know firsthand the issues that plague my own tribe but I found it incredibly insightful to learn about all my relations. This class only emphasized what has been instilled in me from an early age: that we as Native tribal nations are sovereign peoples who have our own distinct beliefs that distinguish us from one another but share a collective consciousness that unifies us culturally. We as Indigenous peoples face a multitude of issues that vary among tribes, yet we still share the same collective struggle, that of recovery. The course taught me that we must overcome the systemic oppression forced upon us and rid ourselves of our colonial ties.

All of this may sound radical and abstract in the context of life at the university but I felt a direct correlation to how I was feeling at school outside of the campus Native community. I definitely felt an overarching sense of being ostracized from my peers and professors and a general disconnect from what I was studying. It was a clash of two worlds for me. I was coming to understand that I was majoring in something that has been used for centuries as the justification for capitalism, which has destroyed my people historically and is keeping us oppressed now. Yet at the same time I was taking courses like Contemporary Issues in an attempt to decolonize my mind by being exposed to the true narrative of my people. I had a lot of inner turmoil but the dots were starting to connect inside and outside of the university setting.

This class served as my long, strong piece of fiber being worked in and out of basket, giving it color, strength, and a glance at the beauty yet to come.

My third year of school—like Harry Potter's—was starting to get intense and I was changing rapidly. It has definitely been my most pivotal year of school. It was the year that would be the straw that broke the camel's hump and would eventually push me towards leaving economics and majoring in ethnic and women's studies. In the early months of that school year I was able to accompany Dr. Dixon and other Cal Poly Pomona faulty to present at the annual National Indian Education Association conference held in Anchorage. It was my first experience leaving the lower forty-eight and traveling outside of the three local states I had been to before. I would have never imagined myself, a young Indigenous boy from Gardena, being able to travel to the last frontier to speak on a panel in front of esteemed university professors and faculty from across the United States and Canada about my experience as a mentor, and have it paid for by the school. I have never been so grateful in my life to be able to travel the way I did that October.

It was also during this year that I was formally appointed student community liaison and took on the task of being the point of contact for Native students on and off campus. I also aided Dr. Dixon in running our newly opened pipeline office, a workplace and student center accessible to those at Cal Poly involved with the summer pipeline program. Through all this work I was, to my own surprise, recognized as a Diversity Champion for the school year. Along with a handful of others, I received an award from the university for my commitment and hard work in bringing diversity to the campus. It was an amazing event and I'm proud to say the Native American Student Center was fortunate enough to host it for the campus community. I felt honored to be the Native recipient for that year.

Despite all this happiness and joy, that school year was my most miserable yet. I began to really hate economics and what it represented to me. An interesting culmination of what I'm sure seemed like trivial events to the professor caused me to finally leave the department and head where my heart truly desired. One day during one of my upper division economics courses, my professor asked the class an open-ended question about monopolies: "What kind of monopolies do the Navajos have?" Someone immediately raised their hand and said casinos and the professor responded no. I decided to give my two cents since I think I know a thing or two about Native Americans and didn't think of the Navajo as too much of a gaming tribe. I replied, "They might have a monopoly on sheep or wool blankets," and to my astonishment my professor turned to me and said, "No they have a monopoly over buffalo hides and arrowheads." He then promptly turned to the class and started laughing and encouraged them to join him. I had never been so humiliated and infuriated in my life at school. After I made a complaint to Irvin at the NASC, which he later relayed to the department, the professor arrogantly still went on to say that he does not need to mind what he says in class because he is a tenured professor and holds a Ph.D. Never in my life had I experienced such blatant racism, stereotyping, and degradation in a class setting, condoned by a university professor.

Soon after, this culmination of events became too much for me and I eventually broke down in front of my mother when I was visiting home one weekend. School had become too much and it was starting to affect other aspects of my life, particularly my mental health. I felt increasingly unhappy with life, especially school. I even debated quitting because I hated it so much at the time. This news of course broke my mother's heart and she felt as if she had failed me when that had not been the case at all. She felt inadequate because she never received an education and couldn't help me in the capacity she felt I needed. She worked six days a week for years to put me through school, but she just didn't have the answers I needed and so she said one of the most powerful things she has said to me in regards to another woman. My mom, sullen with tears, told me go and ask Dr. Dixon for advice because my mom knew she could trust her with my future. I believe this serves as a testament to the quality of faculty and staff we have supporting our Native students on campus. Not only did I have Dr. Dixon to guide me about what to major in and what I could do to properly recover from this incident, I also had the open arms of Irvin Harrison at the student center, who gladly took the time to listen to me voice my complaint and even helped me seek action after the event occurred. He is honest and ultimately cares about the well-being of students. It was such a relief knowing I'd have more than one person to go to who could give me sound advice after something like that. He has not only helped me in times of crisis but helped guide me along my journey through college. Although they are our only two Native faculty, they both go above and beyond to help all of us Native students involved on campus any way they can and I couldn't be any more grateful.

To say the least, I'm more than happy that I left the economics department. Like the fibers of a basket that weave in and out and strengthen the basket's structure and integrity, my professors and peers and the collective college experience have strengthened me, opened my eyes, and helped me become a more aware and socially conscious Indigenous person. I love Cal Poly Pomona and without our Native student support programs I don't honestly know how I would have been able to succeed as an Indigenous person trying to flourish in a system that was not designed for me. And knowing that fact alone makes me enjoy my position on campus, cherish the work I'm able to do in the community, and feel thankful to those who have helped me get to where I am today, no matter how small or trivial it may seem.

My mother always told me that the first thing you make, you should always give it away as a gift to another. I hope the unfinished basket I am weaving can be given to all my relations. My basket, like myself, is a work in progress, a beauty in the making striving to improve things for us all. I someday hope to reciprocate the good that has been done unto me and help someone like myself who struggled but had the support network to push through. I thank all those who have helped me along the way and bid good luck to all those others weaving their first basket.

PETROGLYPHS

DEBORAH A. MIRANDA

All my life, I knew I would disappear. I knew my presence here on earth was so tentative that I was in constant danger of being devoured, absorbed, vanished.

So from the time I could hold a crayon, I scribbled. I scrawled. My hand grew cramped and tired, calluses formed on my fingers from holding a pen, a pencil. I gripped my writing utensil with four fingers instead of three, used my pinky to support the others. Gripped so hard my fingers hurt but couldn't stop. Couldn't stop, because if I did, I would disappear. Everyone I loved had disappeared. I knew I was next.

But if I could keep marking my presence on the earth, on tables, on scrap paper, if I could keep telling the story, if I could keep making words on the page tell the story, then maybe I could hang on.

It wasn't that my world was full of emptiness and nothingness. No, my world wasn't barren. That might have almost been a relief. My world was too full—of violence, abandonment, a mother who didn't come home, fathers who kept disappearing, siblings who were there one day, gone the next. Homes disappeared. Neighborhoods, friends, schools, teachers, friends. Everything in my life disappeared all the time. Why should I be any different? Why had I not disappeared? It was only a matter of time. I knew it.

I remember the first word I ever wrote. On a brown paper bag, with a red crayon. **D E B Y**. I sat at my grandmother's kitchen counter in a red cabin with white trim, high in the Tehachapi Mountains. How can I put this into words you'll understand? Armageddon had already happened. I was three years old. My father had been incarcerated at San Quentin, serving a sentence of eight years. My mother had run away. My two older siblings were put into foster care. I had been taken from the apartment we lived in, and I never saw it again. I never saw my babysitter again. I never saw our furniture, our dishes, our silverware, our blankets, our life again. Every single familiar thing in the world had disappeared.

(Except for my grandmother, my grandfather, and this little red cabin up in the mountains. And even that, my bedrock, my haven, would soon be taken away when I was sent to live with my aunt and uncle. I didn't know until I was thirty years old that although my grandmother wanted to keep me, my grandfather said no. Even at thirty, I learned: there are many ways for people to disappear.)

I held the paper bag out to my grandmother, who was at the sink washing up. We had probably just had lunch; I was allowed to eat sandwiches at the counter, but dinner was always at the table. Tepa wasn't there; maybe outside working on the boat, or the trailer, or the garage, or his fishing gear. It was safe in Mommer's kitchen. The pine paneling, the sunshine streaming in, the mountains all around us, holding us. It seemed I'd always known this place: as a six-month-old baby, I'd contracted a severe case of chicken pox; my mother and siblings were miserable with the disease, but I was listless, thin, and needed special care. My father had brought me here, left me so he could go to work. My grandmother bathed me in that stainless steel sink with cool baking-soda water, held me in her hands, far away from chaos and calamity.

So now, years later, I showed her my name, written in big shaky proud letters. **D E B Y**. That was how my mother had spelled it, how everyone spelled it. That was how I'd learned it. Little red sticks and a few shaky curves, lined up in the right combination, in the correct direction, each one performing a necessary task.

I'm sure my grandmother was proud of me. I'm sure she praised me. I'm sure I'd been practicing. But that moment: that's when I made a transformative leap in my understanding of being. It was as if, when I wrote those letters, made a written record of my self, my name, my existence, those letters grew roots and plowed down through that Formica countertop, into the wooden floor, beams, and concrete foundation of the cabin, deep into the heart of the Tehachapi Mountains themselves.

I had staked myself to this world. I had created a space for myself. I had claimed my fierce life in four little letters. **D E B Y**.

And the potency of those letters was that even when I was far away from this peaceful place—highways and stop signs and back-seats and long hot naps away from these mountains—the waxy strokes of those letters, my name, the ability to muscle my way into reality, into existence, came with me. Always connected me to that mountain, that cabin, the pungent sage on the mountainsides, the sandy earth, dry heated winds, scorching sun, cold blue nights pierced by silver stars.

From that day on, every time I put pencil to paper, I recreated that moment when I came into being. I learned how to carry myself in the world even when nobody else could. It was powerful magic for a little girl. It could have carried me off. Under other circumstances, to touch such power might have burnt me up. But I needed this magic. I needed every single ounce in order to survive what had already happened, what was to come.

In that cusp of time on the mountain, I had to learn fast. The world outside the mountain was a tar pit, a black hole, and my entire family had been swallowed up in it; right down to the last black bobby pin on my mother's head. I was the sole survivor. And although I didn't understand why, and although I grieved silently for all that I had lost, I did not want to follow. I wanted to live.

I have always been drawn back to that mountain, to that brown, stony land. I have dreams in which I simply stand on the porch, look up into the black mass of mountain that stood behind the cabin, and above that shadow, the piercing white constellations of summer.

There is a kind of physical strength that comes to people in moments of extraordinary need—the ability to lift a car off a child, push aside obstacles, pull someone back from a cliff. Fueled by adrenaline, desire, need, often the sudden surge of strength is gone, never to return again, as soon as the emergency is over. I think writing came to me like that. Power came to me in those mountains. Power was visited on me. Power was given to me. And at the same time, I called it. I reached out to it. I found it. Because I was searching. Because I was desperate. Because I knew that black hole was oozing up behind me, lapping at my heels, coming to swallow me up, too. Unlike physical "hysterical strength," however, writing never left me.

DEBY. When I lifted my red crayon from the paper bag, I had earned the magic. I didn't understand it, I hadn't mastered it, but I had touched it, tasted it. And it was good. I could breathe again. I knew where I was. I knew how to keep myself there. I knew how to beat back Disappear.

That red crayon: my wand, my staff, my paint, my ocher, the material that made it possible for my voice to materialize outside of my body. I knew how to say, "I am here." I knew that as long as I kept writing, I would stay here.

This magic has worked for over forty years now. I have a big green plastic footlocker padlocked shut, filled with words, testimony, glyphs, chronicles of those years. I have hauled that footlocker, in various forms, back and forth across the North American continent several times, up and down the West Coast, needed those journals for something, some validation of my continued survival. Along the way I have married, borne children, buried both grandparents and mother, then father, divorced, been in love, found sisters, battled the disease of disappearance at every turn. If I'm not a good wife, I'll disappear. If I'm not a good mother, I'll disappear. If I'm not a good daughter, I'll disappear. If she doesn't love me, I'll disappear.

I journaled my way through it all, and I still do. This essay started in a journal.

But recently, I realized that I am ready to let go of those old journals now. They are just words. No matter how I try to preserve them, the words will fade. Lead markings will soften, ink will lighten. Paper will crumble. Water will seep in, soak apart wood fibers, bleed colors. Like the ancient petroglyphs of my Esselen and Chumash ancestors, my journals are subject to wildfires, floods, lightning strikes, vandalism, time.

I am no longer dependent on making a mark on a piece of paper to know that I am alive, not disappearing, not swallowed up by the horrific unknown that once pursued me. It was good power that I learnt, but there are other ways to use it than to just hold on. It kept me alive, but now . . .

Now I am what is behind the markings on paper. I paint my sunburst on the thin wall of a rock shelter, transfer my power from my body to a symbol. Create a thing from no thing.

And then I release it, walk away, leave it there for you to find—a bright handprint, or faded shadow, or just the hint of spirit animal. I'll wear away, too. Rock faces flake and chip, mosses dissolve pigment, rain releases minerals that streak and stain. I'll return to the elements that created me. But through this mark you will know I was here, and I know you are coming after me. We have stories to exchange about this difficult gift, life, and those stories will never disappear.

PLACE, NATURE, AND WELLNESS

SAGING THE WORLD

ROSE RAMIREZ AND DEBORAH SMALL

A fire went through our family's sage gathering ground, and maybe five acres of white sage just burned to the ground. I was upset, but my uncle said, "It's good—the world just needed saging off."
—*Tima Lotah Link (Šmuwič Chumash)*

Ah, the ubiquitous white sage, Salvia apiana, *a plant that we adore. We use it for ceremony, gifting, food, and medicine. We burn it to cleanse our bodies, minds, ceremonial instruments, and our homes. We use it to help bury our dead and to get us through menopause. From a single leaf to a dried bundle, many of us grow it and have it on hand, ready for use, to gift or to provide to a person in need.*
—*Rose Ramirez (Chumash/Yaqui descent)*

For Barbara Drake (Tongva), white sage is sacred. "White sage is used as a prayer plant. We do not sell white sage. If you need it as a medicine, we're going to give it to you."

A white sage tea is used for bladder ailments or to wash infected sores. "White sage is a very, very powerful antibacterial," according to Julie Cordero-Lamb (Coastal Band of the Chumash Nation). "It's what doctors refer to as a broad-spectrum antimicrobial."

To the general population, white sage is often considered a ceremonial herb, but California Indians have many sacred plants. "For the Luiseño people, elderberry is considered the most sacred . . . not white sage," Willie Pink (Luiseño/Cupeño) tells us. "We counted twenty-seven uses for elderberry."

A plant is often considered sacred because it provides people with something needed, not just because it's used in a ceremony.

Tribes including Kumeyaay, Luiseño, Cupeño, Cahuilla, Chumash, and Kiliwa, among others, have used white sage for thousands of years. Seeds from a variety of sages—black sage, chia, thistle sage, hummingbird sage—are an important food source.

Craig Torres (Tongva) sees plants this way: "Plants are not just 'cultural resources.' Plants are our relatives. They're to be treated with reciprocal respect."

But where does white sage come from? Southern California, from Santa Barbara County to Baja California, from the coastal ranges to the edges of our deserts. Sage scrub and chaparral plant communities provide important habitat for birds, insects, and other animals, several of which are rare, threatened, or endangered, in part due to their disappearing habitat.

But have you noticed that white sage is sold everywhere? If you have traveled through the Southwest, every trade shop sells it, from a small basket of sage to overflowing shelves of small and large bundles, priced accordingly. Often abalone shells are sold alongside the sage. It's also sold all over the country in museum gift shops, bead stores, and businesses on Indian reservations. New Age shops are a prime source, often encouraging pseudo-Native ceremonial use, sometimes providing a prayer or chant to say while smudging.

So how has white sage become so popular, so trendy? Beginning in the 1950s with the urbanization of Native Americans through government work training programs (a.k.a. assimilation and relocation), many Native families ended up in cities like Los Angeles. White sage, similar in many ways to sagebrush and other plants used in their ceremonies back home, was adopted by urban Indians because it was easy to find in Southern California. Its use then spread throughout Native America and attained a pan-Indian status.

In California, some people who were part of the hippie movement of the 1960s co-opted the use of white sage from Native Americans. As the hippie movement evolved into the New Age movement, use of white sage exploded. Now that the market for white sage is international, it's likely that more non-Natives than Native Americans use this herb. White sage smudging is popularized in movies and television. Articles on the benefits of smudging and cleansing pop up daily in newspapers and magazines, as well as on blogs, Facebook, Instagram, and other social media sites, mainstreaming its use.

It is important to note that non-Native people have been using white sage in pseudo-Native ceremonies at least since the 1960s. Yet Native Americans were not allowed to legally practice their religions until the Native American Religious Freedom Act was passed in 1978 (amended in 1994).

Buying and selling white sage is a controversial issue in Native communities. Weshoyot Alvitre (Tongva) tells us, "I was raised with teachings that medicine is not sold. Period." This plant, as with many others, is a medicine, whether used as cure for an ailment or in a ceremonial practice.

The co-opting of Native culture and the continued destruction of white sage stands are a form of cultural appropriation. Alvitre terms it genocide. The voices of Alvitre and the Meztli Project, an Indigenous arts and culture group, have been heard by Anthropologie, which was selling white sage products and pseudo-Native ceremonial kits. In response, the company removed the products from their stores.

Other stores continue to sell white sage. Julia Bogany (Tongva) tells us, "Last year, I went shopping at World Market. I got all the way up to the cash register when I saw sage and sweetgrass. I just threw down all my stuff. That's what we're telling our people to do. Don't! Don't even shop in those stores that are selling white sage. It only empowers them."

The white sage fields are now sacrifice zones for the reckless global commodification of the plants. Hall Newbegin is the founder of Juniper Ridge, one of the largest companies selling white sage on Amazon and Walmart, as well as in stores around the globe. Juniper Ridge gathers all of its white sage for their products from the "wilds of the West Coast."

In "The Sustainability of the Juniper Ridge White Sage Harvest," Newbegin exonerates himself and his company as he scathingly condemns "the free-for-all that's happening in the big sage fields in the Los Angeles basin." His is an eyewitness account:

> I've been harvesting white sage for almost twenty years now, I'm probably one of a dozen people in the world who knows all the harvesting crews, harvesting spots, who the good players are and who are the bad ones. . . . I know this stuff backwards and forwards. . . .
>
> The crews that clear-cut the white sage fields needs [*sic*] to be stopped—I know their bosses are driving them to do it because they want cheap sage; I know both their bosses and the crews; I've brought it up with them in the fields. It's grody, and it needs to stop and it is clear that more monitoring of the open-land fields is necessary, as they are just getting totally hammered, all for a marketplace that's hungry for seven-dollar smudge sticks.

Newbegin goes on to warn us: "You should always be skeptical of us business types. I am always deeply suspicious when biz types say 'oh yeah, of course we have your best interests at heart. . . . I'm in business to make money—ha! I'd be a liar if I didn't own up to this."

Juniper Ridge, the "ultimate hipster bath and body brand," according to product design coach Lela Barker, sells a myriad of white sage products, including essential oils, body lotion, incense sticks, candles, soap, perfume, cologne, and smudge bundles, in stores in Helsinki, Taipei, Barcelona, Sydney, Zurich, San Francisco, Bordeaux, Kraków, Oslo, Berlin, New York, Montreal, Los Angeles, Stockholm, etc., etc., etc. You can check out their online global store locator.

Juniper Ridge seduces us with great photography and design and shares stories about the camaraderie around campfires under starlit skies, getting tipsy on whiskey or bourbon and beer, and stories about travelling to many destinations along California's coast, where sage is just waiting for biz types to gather it, year after year after year.

White sage harvesters are not only from California. According to the late Bert Wilson of Las Pilitas Nursery, "Most of the stuff sold in the upscale trendy places was ripped out of the wild; whole hillsides stuffed into an old van and driven to San Francisco or Seattle or even New York so people can experience something."

When Willie Pink spoke with us, he expressed anger about a particular company in New Mexico: "They send out their harvesters [to California] and they absolutely destroy the plants. They don't care because they're also extracting the white sage oil now. So they'll cut the plants all the way to the ground." Huge quantities of plant material are required to produce even small amounts of essential oils.

Ron Goodman, a San Bernardino County ranger, and Luis Vaquera, a Rancho Cucamonga park ranger, are passionate advocates for the protection of the North Etiwanda Preserve. Located in Rancho Cucamonga, the region is important to many tribes, including Tongva, Serrano, Cahuilla, and Luiseño. The preserve was established in large part through the efforts of the Spirit of the Sage Council, cofounded by Tongva elders Vera and Manuel Rocha.

The rangers spoke to us of the wholesale and on-going poaching of white sage: "Come April, May, and June, it's almost an every-day occurrence. . . . They're taking it when it flowers." The rangers' largest bust last year was almost 1,000 pounds of white sage, stuffed into at least 10 over-sized duffel bags. They've even caught poachers working for seed companies, and they confiscated 150 pounds of white sage seeds (and sage pods) in one bust.

Everyone takes their job seriously at the preserve. Even the sher-iff's deputies get involved in the chase, sometimes using a helicop-ter and a bloodhound to track the poachers across the sage scrub. According to Goodman and Vaquera, at the bottom of the white sage supply chain are often exploited workers who don't know the laws: "They bring these folks up here that have no idea whatsoever that they're committing a crime. . . . All the guys that we catch, they're working for somebody. They get paid twenty-five cents to a dollar per pound." The wholesale value, according to the US Forest Service, is "anywhere from twenty to thirty dollars a pound" as you go up the supply chain a few steps.

For Heidi Lucero (Acjachemen), the foraging of white sage is now "out of control." Craig Torres tells us, "If we don't fight to protect the plants and to protect the land, they're no longer there for us. The connection to who we are as a people has everything to do with the plants." Craig calls the reckless exploitation of white sage trafficking. Bill Madrigal (Cahuilla) refers to it as poaching. So does Lorence Orosco, manager of the Haramokngna/Pukúu Cultural Center.

Lisa Novick of the Wild Yards Project writes that the world is "in the initial throes of a sixth mass extinction, this one caused by people erasing native habitat and negatively impacting the biosphere

. . . foraging native plants is not just irresponsible: it is tantamount to ecocide."

Juniper Ridge claims their wild sage is sustainably foraged from private land. Mike Evans, from Tree of Life Nursery, counters, "If it's public land or if it's private land, it's still habitat."

In her cover story for the *Journal of Medicinal Plant Conservation*, Susan Leopold, executive director of United Plant Savers, writes that the "only sustainable white sage would be white sage that is intentionally grown." White sage is now on the United Plant Savers' To Watch list, a list of the species of important medicinal plants most impacted by human activities.

White sage once grew in what is now the most developed and populated areas in Southern California. Sage scrub and chaparral plant communities continue to be decimated by development. According to the Audubon Society, as little as 10 to 15 percent of California's original coastal sage scrub has survived. Naomi Fraga, director of conservation programs at Rancho Santa Ana Botanic Garden (RSABG), tells us that "coastal sage scrub is now considered a habitat of critical concern."

Also of critical concern are the beautiful iridescent abalone shells that are now marketed, along with white sage bundles and feathers, as smudging kits. You can find hundreds of online sites and stores selling these kits. It's trendy. It's also disrespectful. And extremely painful.

There are seven species of abalone in California. For millennia, they have been crucial to the culture of coastal Native tribes for food, artwork, regalia, adornment, and ceremony. Perhaps most importantly, abalone is part of the creation story for many Southern California tribes. In the traditional story of Chinigchinix, as related by James R. Moriarty in *Chinigchinix: An Indigenous California Indian Religion*: "The people decided to kill Wiyot so they poisoned him. When he realized it he came down to the sand and his mother, the Earth, wanted to cure him and had Wiyot urinate in an abalone shell and she added worms and herbs. While it was fermenting, Coyote came and kicked the abalone shell. The urine became the sea, and that is why it is salty and bitter and the worms became the fish, and the herbs became the kelp." According to the National Marine Fisheries Service, two of the seven California abalone species are now listed as endangered and three listed as species of concern. Poaching, overfishing, and climate change are part of the mix contributing to the devastation of abalone.

We don't encourage buying smudge kits and abalone shells. However, there are a few sustainable growers of white sage: Strictly Medicinal Seeds and Oshala Farm, both in Oregon, and Sagewinds Farm in Jacumba, east of San Diego. We visited Sagewinds. The owners, Ken Taylor and Ellen Woodward-Taylor, have been growing white sage for fifteen years. "I just knew that there wasn't enough for everybody, because there was such a demand," Ellen said. They started with a patch growing on their land, collecting seeds and propagating them. The couple thought it would make a good business and would not deplete the natural sage stands. Sagewinds is now certified organic.

How can we save what remains of our white sage stands? We need to stop supporting the illegal market. Heidi Lucero realized that the sage was being illegally taken from the land and that climate change and development were taking a toll. She stopped gathering from her Acjachemen community's remaining traditional sites. "If you live in California, there's no need to wild gather. Grow your own! Save your ten dollars on a sage bundle and buy a plant that gives you sage all year long." Her sage grows abundantly and she gladly shares it: "My friends probably come over four or five times a month to gather from my plants."

For Theresa Richau (San Gabriel Mission Band of Indians), "plants are important in maintaining a sense of place and belonging. I gather plant materials from native plant gardeners in exchange for my Native Roots products, where I handcraft small quantities of soaps, salves, and lotions, and distill my own line of hydrosols."

To stem the accelerating loss of habitat, growing white sage and other native plants for ourselves and to share with our communities is one of the most beneficial things we can do as individuals. Cultivating white sage and other California native plants is "essentially repatriating those plants back to the landscape from which they grew," according to Naomi Fraga.

We hope you'll join us in cultivating white sage in your garden or nurturing the plants in containers on decks, porches, and windowsills—wherever there is space and sun, and a desire to honor and use the plants.

You can purchase seeds and plants from native plant nurseries throughout the state, including Tree of Life, Theodore Payne, Moosa Creek, RSABG, and local California Native Plant Society chapters, as well as many other reputable growers (see calscape.org).

You'll attract and support bees, butterflies, birds, and other beneficial insects. You'll have the opportunity to spend quality time observing plant and pollinator habitats and better understand how our species' health and well-being are inextricably connected with that of the plants that sustain us.

The sage really needs a few years of love and knowledgeable attention before the really great medicine shows up. And when it does, there is nothing else like it.
—*Julie Cordero-Lamb*

———

When we started our white sage project, *Saging the World,* it was Rose Ramirez, Deborah Small, and Barbara Drake. Barbara was very concerned about the ongoing development near the North Etiwanda

Preserve. Her concerns were justified. Since the creation of the preserve in 1998, housing and other city developments near the preserve have exploded.

We found that development was not the only problem. White sage at the preserve was supposed to be protected under the agreement made with the agencies involved in the mitigation process. The discovery that thousands of pounds of white sage were being stolen from the preserve and sold to the world was shocking to all of us and particularly painful to Barbara.

We began to put together the story of what was happening with white sage, and we were contacted by journalists who heard of our work and interviewed us. White sage was becoming a viral trend due to internet sales and the popularity of social media. Many people found a niche not just to sell the sage, but to sell Native American culture, or the stereotype of Native American culture, which is apparently popular all around the world.

After we wrote the article for *News,* we prepared a slideshow to educate others about the problems. Our first slideshow was presented at the California Botanic Garden, where our friend David Bryant worked, but when Covid hit, we could no longer do in-person slideshow presentations of *Saging the World.* We decided, along with David and Barbara, that a video would be a great way to reach a wider audience.

The four of us met regularly via Zoom, but before filming could begin, we lost Barbara on November 18, 2020. She was our main inspiration, and we hadn't yet had the opportunity to film her. Barbara had begun this journey with us and we knew she would want us to continue working on this important story to tell the world about what is happening with California white sage and to the people and environment that depend on it.

We became filmmakers. David and his partner Neal Uno invested in good equipment to film, record, and interview. Then David began a new job in Sacramento with the California Native Plant Society (CNPS). CNPS joined us in our efforts. We filmed people who shared with us their love and concern for white sage as well as their knowledge of the harmful effects of cultural appropriation on Native people and the environment. Many have worked for decades to protect white sage, but had not yet realized the effects of social media and the internet that has sent poaching into hyperdrive. They have seen the effects on their traditional gathering areas and now are cultivating their traditional plants for personal use and for their communities.

THE G-O ROAD: THIRTY YEARS LATER

CUTCHA RISLING BALDY

S tanding before the Supreme Court on November 30, 1987, Marilyn Miles, representing the Northwest Indian Cemetery Protective Association (NICPA), began her oral argument in a clear and factual manner: "Mr. Chief Justice, and may it please the Court: while I will be addressing two specific points this morning, I would first like to clarify some of the factual discussion that preceded my presentation."

At the time, Miles was a recent graduate of UC Davis Law School and directing attorney for California Indian Legal Services (CILS). Ten years after her work on this case, Miles would go on to become the first woman superior court judge in Humboldt County, where she would serve until she retired in 2017. Her representation of NICPA before the highest court in the land was one of her first

---

Acknowledgments and references for this essay can be found in the References and Notes section at the back of the book.

federal cases and it tasked her with defending one of the most sacred and spiritual areas of northwest California, which local tribes called the High Country.

Lyng v. Northwest Indian Cemetery Protective Association (1988) made headlines in national and international arenas. It arose from several California Indian tribes protesting the building of a road between Gasquet and Orleans in Northern California (known as the G-O Road). The sacred spaces, geological and ecological formations, and ongoing practice of traditional ceremonies in the High Country were of little concern to the Forest Service. They had already built paved sections in the region and now all they needed to connect Gasquet to Orleans was to pave the six-mile section that ran through the High Country. While the case culminated in the 1987 Supreme Court arguments, it had been fought for many years before through grassroots organizing and lower court cases that had all sided with Native tribes and upheld an injunction that stopped the building of the road.

Marilyn Miles's oral argument followed those already made by Andrew J. Pincus, the lawyer representing Secretary of Agriculture Richard E. Lyng, the named petitioner in the case. Pincus argued that the G-O Road was part of an "improved road network" necessary for a timber harvesting program and "for other purposes" and he explained that while the Forest Service's own commissioned report had found "construction of the road would eliminate the required natural conditions and would, therefore, seriously damage the Indians' religious beliefs," in the opinion of the Forest Service, "completion of the road was very significant to the development of timber and recreational resources in the area." Pincus noted that the Forest Service had "reconciled" the potential damage to Native religious freedom by "determining to go ahead with the construction of the road, but to do so in a manner that minimized the intrusion upon the Indians' religious interests."

Miles's arguments were straightforward and tried to clarify the ongoing use of the High Country by Native peoples and how the G-O Road would irreparably damage and disturb the area. In response to a question from Justice Sandra Day O'Connor, Miles explained the importance of the G-O Road case as it stood before the court: "What is happening in this case, Your Honor, which is equally serious, is that these practices go to the very core of the religion for a substantially large number of people, and if they cannot be conducted, if they have that same type of belief, but you physically would be terminating this particular religion for these people by allowing the government to act out in a very public way."

She continued in response to Justice Byron R. White: "We submit, Your Honor, that if the First Amendment means anything, it means that the government cannot take away the very ability of an individual to practice his religion at the only place that it can be practiced under the tenets of their religion. If, indeed, you protect all religions under the Constitution, then this type of site-specific religion is entitled to protection when it is seriously threatened by government action."

The Supreme Court ultimately sided with the Forest Service and, in a five-to-three decision, upheld the right of the Forest Service to build the road. It was a blow to the grassroots and local Native activists who had fought for years to protect the area. The issues with the G-O Road were ultimately settled legislatively, although it required that the area be declared wilderness so that it could be included in the Smith River Protection Act (1990). The case ultimately highlighted the colonial-based legal fictions relied on by the Supreme Court and federal Indian law. It demonstrated the precarious nature of sacred site protection, the free exercise of religion, and the First Amendment, and also the continued challenges to Native American culture and sovereignty. Pawnee scholar Walter Echo-Hawk names the case as one of the "ten worst Indian law cases ever decided" in his book *In the Courts of the Conqueror*. He notes: "After *Lyng*, no constitutional principle exists to protect Native worship on the holy ground located on public land. . . . The *Lyng* ruling leaves American holy places at the complete mercy of the federal government and lets agencies destroy them with constitutional impunity. Under this loophole in religious freedom, there is no enforceable legal protection for this universal form of worship at holy places in the American legal system."

"We were very proud of Marilyn," said Joy Sundberg in an interview with Humboldt State University student Marlene' Dusek (Payómkawichum/Ipai) in 2018. Sundberg, a citizen and former tribal chair of the Trinidad Rancheria, was an active part of NICPA. She also attended the Supreme Court arguments: "When we went in we had to be very quiet. They didn't allow any pencils or pens or paper." Sundberg laughed when she remembered trying to explain to her children what it was like. "You had to be alert and listen to everything."

Sundberg was one of the early members of NICPA. She explained, "I got involved with NICPA because nobody wanted to do it, and so it had to be done, and so I didn't know anything, because I didn't graduate from any school or do anything. I was at home raising kids. I went to the meetings and I had to sit for a long time and I had to read everything." In his book *Grave Matters: Excavating California's Buried Past*, Tony Platt traces the history of NICPA from its founding by organizer Milton Marks (Yurok) and his sister Margaret Marks Lara (Yurok). The original organization also included Milton's daughters Diane and Sandy. Margaret's son, Walt Lara Sr., would also become an active member of NICPA. Platt writes, "As a tag-team, Milton and Walt were a match for any opponents: 'I would strong-arm them, then Milton would smooth-talk them,' says Lara.'"

While NICPA was named in the case, many additional grass-roots activists, artists, and tribal peoples fought on the ground to stop the building of the G-O Road. Today many of the G-O Road activists continue to fight for the sovereignty and self-determination of Native peoples. And while the case, now thirty years old, resulted in a disappointing finding by the Supreme Court, there is no denying the legacy of resistance that those who fought against the G-O Road have left for future generations. The fight to preserve the High Country showed the ongoing connections that Native people have with their lands and the responsibilities they carry to protect these sacred areas.

Students at Humboldt State University have been working with me, my fellow Native American studies professor Kayla Begay (Hoopa Valley Tribe), and special collections librarian Carly Marino to document and create an online archive of materials about the G-O Road. These items will be publicly available on a website to help people explore the history and continued impact of the case. The archive features documents like letters from ceremonial leaders, written by hand, that ask for protection of the High Country. It also features a journal kept by Karuk artist and activist Julian Lang, who participated in the protests and fight against the G-O Road. In one of his journal sketches he wrote, "Protect Indian Religion. NO-GO. Fix the Earth. NEVER SAY I'M NOTHING. If you fix the Earth you ARE somebody! Stop the Gasquet-Orleans Road in Northern California. STOP THE ROAD."

In an interview with Dusek in 2018, Lang remembered, "My role was kind of like the community awareness kind of thing. I guess what my job was, I actually ended up being the fundraiser so we were able to raise a lot of funds. And also to kind of be spokesperson." Lang recalled, "We used to have these incredible gatherings and every couple of months we'd have a big public meeting on what's going on, we might have two to three hundred people there. . . . We had all kinds of community and support for this thing called the High Country."

Chris Peters (Puhlik-lah/Karuk), now the president of the Seventh Generation Fund, was also an instrumental part of the G-O Road case. In the federal district court lawsuit, he had been one of the named plaintiffs alongside NICPA; Jimmie Jones, Sam Jones, and Lowana Brantner were the others. Echo-Hawk describes Peters as a lead witness in the case. His testimony, along with that of other witnesses, helped sway the district court judges who sided with the Native peoples and stopped the road. The Supreme Court ruling would ultimately overturn these decisions. Peters, who has spoken about the case in various venues, did an interview with KHSU in 2018 about the importance of Native activism and why this case was so historic:

> The progress of the G-O Road was an awakening, a moving away from the threat of massacres. And our spiritual leaders, our thinkers, our philosophers, were again able to have the freedom to look around and say this is where we are situated, what are we going to do about it? And all of a sudden the G-O Road case erupted. The plan devastated the ability for Native Peoples to actualize a spiritual belief system and that ability impacted ceremonial life and impacted traditions and philosophies. What was wrapped in the G-O Road was the final phase of cultural and spiritual genocide being perpetrated by the federal government.

In a contemporary context, fights for sacred sites, land use, and protection of water and natural resources continue to make headlines as Indigenous peoples around the world lead the way in environmental justice. 2018 marked thirty years since the G-O Road case, which continues to have lasting impacts, reflected in numerous citations in scholarship, law, art, research, and legislation. There are still ongoing fights to protect the use and stewardship relationship of Native peoples to sacred places on public lands. And there is also a deep, lasting inspiration from the activism surrounding the G-O Road case that motivates new and future generations.

Sundberg still remembers when the Supreme Court read their decision after she and many others in the Northwest California region had fought so hard to protect the High Country. "I thought, maybe it was a waste of time for us to go there. The white man will do what he wants to do, and it's just like the people said over here, Joy, don't go because they are going to do what they want to do about it, period. And they did." But, she explained, "It wasn't popular at that time to be an Indian but I always thought, well, we gave our time and we opened a lot of doors for a lot of young people."

WATER AND OIL

MICHELLE L. LAPENA

The Great Central Valley of California used to be a floodplain. It was a marshy wetland before non-Indian settlement began, full of insects and game. Major villages of Native people lived along the banks of what are now the Sacramento and San Joaquin Rivers. The Sacramento River in the north, gathering from its Feather and American River tributaries, flows southward through the valley for over four hundred miles. In the San Joaquin Valley, its namesake flows roughly northwest for almost four hundred miles, picking up its tributaries, the Merced, Tuolumne, Stanislaus, and Mokelumne Rivers. Sadly, over one hundred years, the Central Valley has become a watershed that has been sucked dry of water and oil.

Native people call the Earth our mother, and water is her blood, sacred, flowing, creating a world that humans can live in. Our blood carries oxygen into our bodies, circulating, gathering impurities and waste, carrying them to the organs that can process them, in a loop that has no end until we die. Our mother has a circulatory system as well. It is the water cycle: the air, water, soil, and sun are necessary parts of the system. Water is the source of all life on Earth, yet there is another liquid in the system that humanity does not yet comprehend, and that is oil. It is the decomposing remains of the past, sacred, like water, in the soil.

The soils in the Central Valley are deceptively fertile, as most grassland soils are. The muck that accumulated over time is dense and loamy, with deep-running nutrients. Floodwater churned the soil, turning it with high tides, stirring the feces of animals and decomposing matter. Native grasses grew, lived, went to seed, and died for millennia. Tubers and roots were tilled by the claws of the grizzly and their game, the squirrels, gophers, and weasels. Although most people think of the grizzly only as a predator, it was also Nature's earth mover.

With the eradication of the grizzly, the valley soils were left open to the taking. Native tribes along the rivers, who burned the grasslands to clear it of excess insects and allow for travel, were the target of government-sponsored bounty programs. Early California laws were geared toward clearing the land of "hostile" Indians; the state authorized payments of fifty cents per scalp and five dollars per decapitated head. Fear drove Natives deeper into the hills, opening the valley to non-Indian settlement. The Great Central Valley, a well-tended garden, suddenly lost its caretakers.

The new owners saw the land's potential for agriculture. The water and the elevations were perfectly suited to widespread farming. Within a few decades, land in the San Joaquin Valley was cleared of remnants of what remained from before. Grasslands were turned under and creeks were straightened into ditches. The river was levied and the land was quartered. Everything became straight and flat. Round edges of rivers became cement canals, with gates and meters. Water, once abundant and belonging to no one and everyone, was now property to be bought and sold. Indian land was granted in forty-acre quadrants to the highest bidder.

The rich soils and favorable weather of the 42,000-square-mile Central Valley enticed settlers who were unfamiliar with its natural rainfall patterns, and they began intense irrigated agriculture on the lands that were not as subject to flooding. They soon found themselves troubled by frequent floods in the upper Sacramento Valley and a general lack of water in the lower San Joaquin Valley. The Sacramento River drains the northern half of the state, which receives between 60 and 75 percent of the precipitation in the valley, and flows into the San Joaquin River, which receives only about 25 percent of the rainfall. The Great Central Valley is like a toilet, the bowl filling up in the north and flushing out into the south. Because water was needed for intense, irrigated agriculture in the south, it was sought out in every manner: wells were drilled, canals and reservoirs were built, and government subsidies supported the effort.

As early as 1873, Barton S. Alexander completed a report for the US Army Corps of Engineers, the first attempt at creating a Central Valley water project. Alexander was a military man who graduated from West Point and worked his way up to lieutenant colonel. An engineer by training, he sought to build things that would last and endure like a lighthouse on the rocky Minot's Ledge off the New England coast or the Smithsonian Institution's castle. In his later years, his attention turned to water works in the Central Valley, believing that he could lay the foundation for a new civilization.

In 1904, the Reclamation Service (now the Bureau of Reclamation) latched on to the hope that a complicated water system could work, but a system did not take hold until a series of droughts in the early 1920s. In 1933, the state of California passed a law authorizing the Central Valley Project (CVP), which included the sale of bonds to raise nearly $170 million for the project. However, the bonds were not sufficient and the Great Depression hit the Central Valley around that same time. After much back and forth between the state and the Army Corps of Engineers, the CVP eventually cut through the natural flushing system that created the fertile valley soils. The era of Big Agriculture began.

The first wave of immigrants were now landowners, and new immigrant farm workers became the thread in the fabric, new ones always being added, holding the system together. To make farming profitable, immigrant workers, especially those lacking citizenship, were paid the lowest wages they would accept. To further cut costs, particularly the high cost of water that was delivered through the CVP, the farmers drilled. Drilling rigs found the water table plentiful in the beginning after thousands, if not millions, of years of natural ecological flushing. Water seeps, it creeps and leaks into the tiny crevices between each piece of dust. The molecules of water search for each other underground. The dowsers, drills, and pumps found it wherever it hid below the surface.

In the early days of San Joaquin Valley farming, farmers grew traditional row crops: corn, tomatoes, peas, lettuce, strawberries, onions. But the value of row crops per acre, with the high cost of surface water from the CVP, was dwarfed by the value of permanent crops, including citrus, nuts, and grapes. The Central Valley slowly began to shift away from traditional food crops to high-value export items that came from permanent planting. To cut costs, most landowners continued to search for every drop of groundwater. The water table, once flush with millions of years of water drainage, was tapped out, and the land began to sink.

Today the US Geological Survey estimates that the valley floor is subsiding at an average rate of one to two feet per year. Total subsidence since the early 1900s ranges from twenty-five to forty feet, depending on the location. The Corcoran Clay that protects the deepest aquifers, acting as a filter between the upper and lower waters, is compacting.

Like the hardening of a liver with fatty tissue, the Corcoran Clay is losing its tiny gaps that filter the water, back and forth, through alluvial movements that the human eye will never see. As with cirrhosis, filtering spaces in compacted clay cannot be restored.

What lies beneath is the easiest to forget. Like burials that we walk away from and never see again, most people don't like to think about what is underground. What one cannot see does not exist. But the underworld is a vast system of rivers and tides; it dries and replenishes, flows and ebbs. Without our interference, the system replays the cycles, the seasons of flood and drought and the longer cycles that replenish the system over centuries. We cannot know the centennial patterns because we have already interrupted them. Most of us cannot understand our part in it because we cannot see it.

Driving down Interstate 5 today, one would have difficulty reconciling the history of the great watershed valley with what the eyes see. The skin of the soil hangs from the bones of parallel mountain ranges, a starving cow. Dust whips into devilish whirlwinds between blackened almond and citrus trees. The trees are black with drought, not from fire—as if they are living off the oil being fracked below the surface. The groundwater in the upper levels of the soil is nearly gone. Oil is lighter than water; it rises to the top when given enough space, a crack, a well.

As some farmers drilled ever deeper to water permanent crops, from four hundred feet to over twelve hundred feet in some places, instead of water, they found tarry sands made of compacted compost of millennia. Our mother has another vital fluid in her circulation, oil. The discovery triggered decisions: whether to find water and grow food, or to drill deeper, crack the rock and suck out the oil, frack rock.

Oil production is not new to the San Joaquin Valley. In 1899, "black gold" was discovered in a shallow, hand-dug oil well on the west bank of the Kern River. The Kern discovery triggered an oil boom, and a forest of wooden derricks grew seemingly overnight on the grasslands north of Bakersfield. Kern County oil fields produced a majority of the oil from California, and made it the top oil-producing state in the nation. Like in the gold rush that preceded the Kern River oil discovery, speculators flocked to the San Joaquin Valley and oil fields became as common as farmlands. Gushers at Coalinga, McKittrick, and Midway-Sunset fields kept the pumps going.

The San Joaquin Valley is home to twenty-one giant oil fields, which have produced over one hundred million barrels of oil each. There are also four "super giants" that have each drawn over one billion barrels of oil from the Earth. Oil derricks, many vacant, are fixtures on the landscape, like remnants of an ancient forest. The scent of oil, as moss, hangs from the dead oaks that linger on the low sloping foothills on the oak savannah above the valley floor. The oaks were mighty giants, now fossils, like stone sculptures that only remain for the shade they might give. Their roots cannot process oil. Steam injections into the ground, intended to drive viscous crude oil into the pumps, drives it up though the sandy loam, through the upper mantle. Roots, with their suction, cannot know that the water has turned to oil. The tiny pores pull and seek water from the upper aquifer; instead they grab onto the vapors of steamed oil and carbon dioxide.

The trees may not know that humans have tampered with the ground, needling into unwilling places that can't protect themselves. Oil producers and water purveyors perform surgery on the Earth, not knowing her chances of survival beforehand, never considering whether it should be done at all. It is elective surgery that cannot be undone. The pores in the Corcoran Clay cannot be repaired by injecting new liquid, the subsidence cannot be filled with chemicals, and the billions of gallons of crude oil cannot be replaced with transfusions. To face these facts may be too difficult for many to consider. But ignorance is the one way to guarantee that we will keep doing it, keep pulling from the Earth, not knowing if it will kill the human race in the end. Only a fool, a glutton, or a thrill seeker takes that kind of chance.

Native people believe that we are made from our mother, the Earth. We were created here to be a caretaker. Many of us believe that humans can tend to the land, manage natural resources in a sustainable manner, and preserve the environment by taking responsibility for our actions. The Earth cannot speak in words that people can hear, but she can tell us in other ways, as she is now. She is telling us in storm, in fire, in flood, and in drought—the language that has always told us her needs. We don't always heed her warnings to move to higher ground, or to clear tinder from the forest with controlled burning, or to stop wasting water. We still ignore her message to stop draining her blood made of oil, because it, like water, is sacred.

It is easier to understand the sacred nature of water because humans need it to live. But oil is also from the Earth. When we draw it from her, by steam, pump, or frack, we may be causing an injury that cannot be reversed. Unlike water, which can cycle through the atmosphere and the soil, oil may not be meant to burn. It gathers in places underground for a reason, some reason that humans do not yet understand. Its nature is to coagulate—perhaps it is clotting in places to stop from bleeding out on its own. There are such places where a form of oil, asphalt, or tar rises on its own, such as the La Brea Tar Pits in what is now Los Angeles. In the past, Chumash and Tongva people carefully gathered tar from this resource for waterproofing or glue. The tar pits were a place to be watchful, a scab that protects the air, coagulating tar with the blood of animals.

Oil is known as a fossil fuel because it was formed when the remains of animals and plants from millions of years ago were covered by layers of sand. Heat and pressure from these layers, like deep compost, turns the remains into crude oil. It is a dark liquid that is usually found in natural underground reservoirs, like pockets of glue that hold continents together. When crude oil is burned—for combustion, accidentally, or as a spill control measure—it emits chemicals that affect human health. Exposure to burning crude oil may harm the passages of the nose, airways, and lungs. It may cause shortness of breath, difficulty breathing, coughing, itching, red or watery eyes, and black mucous. It is well established that chemical interactions from burning crude oil can cause illness, including cancer, yet the world we live in is dependent on doing just that.

There are many forms of liquid fuel, including crude oil, asphalt, liquid natural gas, and others. The burning of these compounds has a harmful effect on the human environment. The oxygen that we breathe, the weather that we experience, the amount of rainfall each year, and the overall temperatures that we see changing are all impacted by combusting oil. The mixture of oil and air is an experiment that is well underway, and Nature is telling us in her language the result. But this guidance from Nature on the importance of clean air is not as easy to hear, or to see, as the impact of mixing oil and water.

There are over 230,000 miles of oil and gas pipelines in the United States alone. Only a small fraction of the pipelines are regulated, and there have been over sixteen hundred reported pipeline accidents and leaks since the 1980s. The safety of pipelines is usually analyzed in comparison with trucking or railroad accidents. While those figures are important, more humans are affected by pipeline spills into waterways and the oceans than are killed in cataclysmic accidents. The high environmental cost of oil spills is impossible to calculate because these are events that never occurred in the Earth's prior history. The effect on plants and animals, in real time and over long periods of time, is beyond measure.

The choice between sudden death by an exploding tanker or slow death from cancer might be easy for some. But this is a false choice. The real choices are whether we should be using fossil fuels at all, and if so, how to prevent additional harm to the environment. The protests against the Keystone XL and especially the Dakota Access Pipeline are examples of Native people bringing this question into the mainstream consciousness. It is not easy to explain the complexity of the Earth, the water cycle, and what cannot be seen in the air and underground. Because we live in a social media–driven society now, it has been boiled down to a very simple idea: water is life.

Water is necessary for all life. When NASA explores other planets in far-away galaxies, they look for evidence of water. Without water, there is no habitat suitable for life as we know it. The Earth, our home, has water. Over time, humans have tried to tame it, to capture it, but what many humans fail to consider is that nothing is static. The Earth has dynamic systems that are always moving. The Earth's crust slides and lifts deep under our feet, as we sleep. Water flows underneath us in most places, whether in the upper aquifers or deep inside the Earth's mantle. Nothing stays the same. Subsidence of the valley floor is a force that Barton S. Alexander didn't consider in 1873. He only saw the Earth's surface and tried to make a better water delivery system than our Creator had. But the canals are now broken, the concrete is buckled, and the water is leaking. Nature is more powerful than anything humans can design.

The builders of pipelines, like builders of great canals such as Alexander, seem to forget that the Earth is a living system. They discount that there are underground rivers with ecosystems, plants and animals who move around in their lives under the surface. Everything is moving, shifting, and human activity intersects with those movements. Pipelines are inserted into a living system, one that will expel them, as our bodies push out a splinter. The pipe, no matter the material, will break, spilling its contents into soil, into water. Oil and water do not mix, and Nature is telling us what happens when human intervention brings them together.

More people are affected by the lack of clean drinking water today than in past generations. Whether the contamination is from lead, arsenic, mercury, or chemicals released in an oil spill, the effects on human health are a call for action. As humans, we have some ability to shield ourselves from harm, but plants and animals cannot just move or drink bottled water. Human "dominance" over the rest of Nature, however, ends when our air and drinking water is too contaminated for humans to survive. After all, water and air are the two essential elements for human life.

The caretakers of this land, such as those at the Sacred Stone Camp in North Dakota, are trying to translate a message that many are unable or unwilling to hear. When governments allow the wholesale theft of water and oil for corporate gains, at the expense of our natural environment, and causing the contamination of our air and water, those governments are failing the people they represent. Applying the economic theory of the tragedy of the commons, the #NoDAPL movement is asking us to stop allowing individuals, acting independently and in their own financial self-interest, from behaving contrary to the common good of all users by depleting the resource.

Several decades ago, I was very concerned about development of a ski resort on my tribe's sacred mountain, Mount Shasta, in northeastern California. I was writing about it in *News from Native California* and doing a lot of research. One day, I had what some might call a vision; others might say it was a dream. I was walking up a mountain trail and came upon a small cabin in the woods. An old woman with long white hair cascading down to her feet sat on the porch in a rocking chair. She smiled at me and gestured for me to come closer. As she transformed into the mountain, she told me without words not to worry. She showed me a vision of a violent earthquake—perhaps it was an eruption of the mountain's dormant volcano. She told me not to worry about the ski lifts, saying she would "shake them off, like fleas off a dog." When I woke, I felt relief. Our mother is the one in charge. The Earth is telling us to be watchful, to take heed. But she will continue without us if we are unable to listen.

WATER IS LIFE: THE FLOWER DANCE CEREMONY

CUTCHA RISLING BALDY

"We are what, 70 percent water if we're hydrated? 80 percent? That's what we're doing. We are rearranging the water in your body to be able to hold joy . . . that's how I would characterize it. We're changing the water to be able to hold beauty . . . . That's what singing does for her on a personal level."
—*Melodie George-Moore (Hupa/Karuk)*

It was August 2014 and I was driving up I-5 on my way to the Lewiston Dam near Redding. I was going to meet up with many other Hupa, Yurok, and Karuk people and various supporters in the hopes that the Bureau of Reclamation could be swayed to release additional water flows into our rivers. Earlier that summer, the bureau had announced that there were no plans to augment river flows even though reports from biologists and community organizations

References for this essay can be found in the References and Notes section at the back of the book.

had found the presence of a parasite that could endanger fish and wildlife. This parasite was the same one that had infected thousands upon thousands of fish in the Klamath River in 2002, a result of low water flows and high temperatures.

Over the past few years, the Trinity River has suffered from the constant seizure of water by Central Valley farmers and the state of California and the continued maintenance of the dam that keeps the river unseasonably low, but in good years the river is clear, cool, and a place of great social, spiritual, and cultural importance. The World Renewal ceremonies are held along the river, including a key part, the Boat Dance, which requires that the Hupa navigate down the river in canoes while dancing and singing. For a number of years, because of the continued seizure of water by outside interests, the Hupa have been forced to ask for water to be released so that they can perform this ceremony and help maintain the balance of the world. Over the past few years, our rivers have also had periods where they have become toxic to human beings and animals. In some of the hotter summer months, we have been faced with warnings not to swim in or drink the water from our river. We have also contended with continued threats to our fish and other wildlife.

In the Hoopa Valley we are, without a doubt, salmon people. We are also acorn people. We are also river people. Our river, now known as the Trinity, is called Hun' in our language. But the Trinity River, as a power and place of prayer, is called *ta'na:n-na:niwe:sile'n* or "water-you who have come to flow down through here." Our river runs through the center of our valley, and throughout my life I have heard it referred to as the artery of our land and what keeps us living and thriving. We are, without a doubt, intimately tied to our river, our creeks, our springs, our water. Because water is life. And as so many other Indigenous peoples have known since the beginning of time, we are the water, and the water is us.

That summer when the Bureau of Reclamation announced that it had no plans to augment river flows, the Hoopa Valley Tribe organized a protest at the Lewiston Dam. At the dam I was greeted by a group of young women, many of whom had been *kinahłdung* or Flower Dance girls. We were going to be a part of a large group of people participating in a Flower Dance demonstration where we would sing for our water, not only in the hope that we would call attention to the possibility of another massive fish kill but also to offer prayers to the water, the land, and the people. This strong group of women and men, many of whom are regular participants in our women's coming-of-age ceremony, were an embodiment of our continuing cultures, as well as our determination and strength in the face of overwhelming odds. For a number of years our women's ceremony was not commonly practiced, with some anthropologists and ethnographers going so far as to call it extinct. This does not mean that our coming-of-age ceremony did not remain part of our cultural imagination. Many elders in our tribe would constantly educate and tell stories about our women's ceremony. They saw it as a foundational part of who we are as Hupa people. They continued to sing songs, demonstrate the movements, and talk about the importance of celebrating and honoring young women. After many years of hard work by various women in our tribe, we held our first revitalized Flower Dance ceremony in May of 2001 for Kayla Rae Carpenter (now Begay).

Kayla's mother, Melodie George-Moore, would be the medicine woman for many of these revitalized women's coming-of-age ceremonies. She would help to build up a new generation of young women as they faced a new world, one where they could be strong Hupa leaders, and one that would continue to challenge them with daily acts of colonialism. At the Lewiston Dam, as we gathered to sing and pray for the water, Melodie would lead the way once again. She spoke to the crowd of people and introduced the dance as being an important demonstration not only of the power of women, but also the power of community. And, in a way that had become very poignant and important to Melodie, this dance is also very clearly about water, because water is life.

The contemporary Flower Dance ceremony is usually three, five, or ten days. Each day includes a number of activities where the young woman will learn more about her changing roles, but also about her deep and personal ties to her culture, land, and community. Daily activities include running, steaming, talking circles, ritual fasting, bathing, learning about herbs, and singing, among many others. This ceremony is particularly important to the Hupa as it is thought that each young woman's behavior during these days demonstrates how she is going to live her life. Running in particular demonstrates how she will live her life. If she falls, she must get back up; if she gets tired she must keep going. When she runs, young children chase behind her, sometimes teasing her, trying to get her to turn around—effectively "going back" toward her childhood.

Bathing is also a foundational part of this ceremony and is important for introducing what will become a routine and ritual bathing that is a part of self-care in Hupa culture. During each day of the ceremony the *kinahłdung* runs and does a ritual bath at various bathing spots known as the *tim* (lucky spots). On the last day of the ceremony, she will do a ritual bath in all of the bathing spots. Bathing helps the young woman to become intimately tied to the river, and by extension the land and her community. The river that will nourish the young woman throughout her life provides her with an essential place of prayer during this ceremony. As young women begin preparations for the ceremony, Melodie will sometimes take them down to the river to make an offering, she says, to "begin a sense of place." In an interview that I did with her about the revitalization of this ceremony she told me:

Some girls I've taken down to the water to give offering to the river, as well as to begin a sense of place, because there's a number of things that are helpful to people who are holding space or holding ground against colonization. How do you keep well? And so there's a list of things, I've kind of narrowed it down from this dance . . . that sense of place, somewhere that you can tie yourself to; that's part of what is happening with this girl saying prayers at the river, with these bath spots—she's got a sense of place. That's where home is. That's where I'm tied to right there.

The bathing, the running alongside the river, the intimate ties this young woman builds to her place, this is what will ground her as she moves forward in life. Many of our ceremonies give us an intimate connection to the river, they remind us that we are responsible for our river, our environment. These ceremonies teach us that our well-being is tied to our environment and our community. They teach us that we are intertwined with our world, not separate, not dominant.

When we came to the Lewiston Dam to pray for increased water flows, we were also demonstrating that our prayers, ceremonies, and culture teach us to be diligent, strong, and active. In this modern world we are constantly confronted with attempts to belittle, ignore, or silence our presence on this land, yet we remain ever diligent in our protection of our land, animals, and water, not just for ourselves but for everyone. That day, as our tribal members wore shirts that read "Free Our River," I stood with a group of Hupa people who, despite the more-than-hundred-degree weather, sang as loud as they could, over the sound of rushing water, calling out into the mountains. We sang Flower Dance songs for our water. We sang songs that several years before had been silenced and were now, once again, thriving. "I think about these girls," Melodie told me.

"I think about how they bathe in our river and how it blesses them. I think about how much that means to them, and how much it means to us. Our water is in us."

Over the past several years many of our social media, and in some cases mainstream media, feeds have been filled with the growing Indigenous fight to protect water. Notably, the Dakota Access Pipeline finally became headline news after thousands of Native people and allies went to the Standing Rock Reservation to stop construction of a pipeline underneath the Missouri River. *"Mni Wiconi"* or "Water is Life" became an oft-cited mantra. As they gathered at the various camps, Indigenous peoples from around the world shared their own water songs, dances, and prayers. And I was struck once again by the sheer number of Indigenous voices that could testify to the intimate and ancient ties we have to the water that nourishes this land.

It is through our culture, our languages, our stories, and our ceremonies that we are taught our interconnectedness with the land, environment, animals, and water. And now, nearly two decades after the revitalization of our women's coming-of-age ceremony in Hoopa, we continue to stand as a community of people, alongside our *kinahłdung*, with songs, prayers, and laughter at demonstrations like the one at the Lewiston Dam in 2014. I realized in that moment the level of wellness that we bring to our dances and to ourselves we also bring to our water. We heal ourselves, we heal the water. We heal the water, we heal ourselves.

CALIFORNIA CAN'T PROMISE TRUTH AND HEALING WHILE FORCING THE SALMON INTO EXTINCTION

SAVE CALIFORNIA SALMON

In early spring 2021, it was obvious that California's rivers and salmon people were facing disaster. Forecasts for the Klamath River predicted some of the lowest salmon returns on record and low allocations for tribal fishers. Once snow-peaked, the mountains stood bare and parched. Reservoirs were low from the previous year's water deliveries, which favored industrial agriculture over salmon and tribal people.

California's spring and winter run Chinook and coho salmon were nearing extinction in many watersheds, yet the state was doing little to nothing to preserve water for California's salmon runs, which quickly became casualties of the state's destructive water infrastructure.

Acknowledgments and references for this essay can be found in the References and Notes section at the back of the book.

California was poised to deliver water to agriculture rather than use its own laws to protect reservoir storage and river flows. Salmon and drinking water supplies were threatened as a result of poor water policy and an outdated water rights system.

The conditions created the perfect storm, capable of obliterating already struggling salmon populations. For Native people, the loss of salmon is apocalyptic. Water and salmon are the cornerstone of ceremony, spirituality, sustenance, and physical existence. Scientists have even linked compromised mental health as well as increased diabetes, heart disease, and obesity to dwindling salmon runs.

"What many don't understand is that California is a salmon state and what happens to the salmon happens to us," explained Chief Caleen Sisk, spiritual leader of the Winnemem Wintu Tribe. "What happens to the people if salmon runs are nearing extinction, and if the rivers are dangerously low and full of algae? Not only did Newsom and the state fail to take any actions to protect river storage or river flows in the North State, they actually tried to say that actions like building Sites Reservoir and voluntary agreements for water withdrawals are drought measures. These proposals benefit industrial agriculture, which uses 80 percent of the state's water, not the North State or tribal communities. Salmon benefit us."

The dire state of the salmon, in addition to quickly dwindling reservoir storage, led many tribes and environmental groups to organize actions, lawsuits, and protests. In the past the state chose to let whole broods of salmon die rather than challenge the powerful agriculture industry and deal with its outdated water rights system.

Bad water decisions during the 2014–2015 drought killed over 90 percent of the Sacramento River's winter run salmon babies and eggs, and killed almost all of the Klamath River's juvenile fall Chinook salmon for three consecutive years.

The issue came to a head when the federal government proposed keeping the Trump plan in place for managing the Central Valley

Water project and turned in a temperature management plan to the California State Water Resources Control Board (SWRCB) for the Shasta Reservoir. This plan would let almost 90 percent of the endangered winter run Chinook salmon die. Tribes and environmental groups confronted the State Water Board in public hearings and even turned in an alternate plan for managing diversions from the Shasta and Trinity reservoirs. Ultimately, the state approved the plan, which killed even more winter run Chinook salmon than expected.

Save California Salmon and tribal representatives held a virtual State of the Salmon event in May to inform the public about the looming disaster and the need to take action. At the event Amy Cordalis, attorney for the Yurok Tribe, explained, "Our salmon are in the poorest condition they've ever been in and that's hard as a tribal person to even say, to even acknowledge, because that hurts us to our core. Many people know that the Klamath River was once the third-largest salmon-producing river in the whole West . . . now it's very hard to acknowledge that there are so few fish left."

As spring progressed, the situation worsened. Almost all of the juvenile salmon in the Klamath River began to die from a disease called *Ceratonova shasta*. *C. shasta* is spread by a host parasite that thrives in the low water conditions in dammed watersheds.

Scientists have said that Klamath dam removal would greatly reduce *C. shasta* numbers because the host parasite cannot thrive in flowing rivers. In past years, water has been released to stop the spread of *C. shasta*. This year, 2021, the Bureau of Reclamation denied the Yurok Tribe's request for water releases, leaving many tribal biologists with the morbid job of counting dead salmon.

"I have worked for Yurok fisheries for twenty-three years and extinction was never part of the conversation, but over the last five to seven years there's been an overall decline within the lower basin," Yurok Tribe biologist Jamie Holt said. "We have seen increased water temperatures, longer durations of high temperatures, and lack of river flow leading to disease distribution. These factors led to the large-scale fish kill we witnessed in the spring. If we have another die-off at this level we will be discussing extinction."

Holt explained that the tribe has seen at least a two-thirds reduction in juvenile fish in only a few years due to the juvenile fish kill. She said the *C. shasta* hot zone has gone from a short section of the river to over a hundred miles long, right through the middle of the Yurok reservation. The situation is taking a toll on tribal biologists.

"My feelings are equal parts anger and sadness. As a scientist this is so frustrating, as so many people have called out the mismanagement of the river and said what needs to happen for so long. As a Yurok person I was put here to take care of the fish. I feel like we are really sinking here," Holt said.

Meanwhile, downriver alfalfa farmers in two major salmon tributaries of the Klamath River, the Scott and Shasta Rivers, started irrigating their fields in early spring without the restrictions that federal Klamath Project irrigators faced. River flows dropped quickly. The Shasta River, the only spring-fed tributary of the Klamath below the Klamath dams, is one of the main producers of fall run Chinook salmon, the main salmon run that still feeds the Klamath Basin tribes. The Scott River is the main spawning ground in the Upper Klamath for coho salmon, an endangered species. Most years, both rivers run dry by fall due to uncontrolled water diversions. This year they started going dry in early summer.

The dire situation on the Scott and Shasta Rivers nudged tribal members and local residents to start calling into every California SWRCB hearing and for the Karuk Tribe to file a legal petition requesting that the Water Board take immediate action to curtail irrigation deliveries in the Scott Valley.

"The worst water conditions in history led federal agencies to shut off thirteen hundred farms in the upper basin, but in the Scott Valley water users continue business as usual," said Karuk Chairman

Russell "Buster" Attebery in the statement about why the tribe asked California to curtail water diversions from the Scott River. "They are dewatering the last stronghold of coho salmon in the Klamath Basin, driving them to extinction."

In the Trinity River, the Klamath's largest tributary and the only Klamath River tributary that is diverted into California's Central Valley Water Project, the Hoopa Valley Tribe warned the Bureau of Reclamation that the river was suffering unusually high temperatures and experiencing a toxic algae bloom. The Trinity is normally relied upon as a cool water source offering relief to salmon below its confluence with the Klamath River. This year, adult spring run Chinook salmon that would typically seek refuge in cool tributary waters had few places to go where water temperatures are not lethal. They were crowding at the mouths of creeks, making them vulnerable to disease and predation.

The Klamath-Trinity spring Chinook salmon, which had recently become listed as endangered under state law due to a petition by the Karuk Tribe, were beginning to be affected by *columnaris* (gill rot), the same disease that killed more than sixty-four thousand adult salmon in 2002.

Tribes were able to get a three-day water release to help these springers move before they died. However, as the flows were being released, a comment period on a plan to divert another thirty-six thousand acre-feet of water from the Trinity reservoirs to the Sacramento River closed. This plan threatens future water releases for the Trinity and Klamath salmon and drinking water sources.

"Sending water out of the Trinity River system is bad enough, but to send additional water out of [the] basin during an extreme drought leaves our salmon even more vulnerable," said Allie Hostler, Hoopa tribal member and Save California Salmon advisory board member. "To make it through this dry season, we need to fight to retain at least six hundred thousand acre-feet behind Trinity Dam.

If we don't we could very well see another catastrophic fish kill. Continuing to deplete water storage while big ag gets water deliveries for non-essential crops is not acceptable."

The tribes continue to meet with the Bureau of Reclamation weekly to discuss water conditions and to check temperature and water quality.

"The Hoopa Valley Tribe has fought since time immemorial to retain cold, clean water in the Trinity River," Chairman Joe Davis said. "Although we've won several landmark cases, the pressure continues to rise as we see our salmon's health dwindling and more demand for our cold, clean water. We are prepared to continue our fight and keep Trinity River water in the Trinity River system."

As the fight for California's water raged on, the Winnemem Wintu Tribe began preparations for their three-hundred-mile Run4Salmon from the McCloud River above the Shasta Reservoir to the San Francisco Bay. This year the run followed the journey of the outmigration of young salmon as they struggled for survival, and included a Trinity River connection run.

"Run4Salmon is a way to get people onto the water, to see how the water is treated, where it is exported, and to help people think outside the box about water," explained Chief Caleen Sisk of the Winnemem Wintu Tribe. "Many people think the water is exported for drinking water, but it is not, it is mainly diverted to industrial agriculture, which continues to expand. These are not farmers feeding Americans, it is big ag, exporting crops like almonds. Our salmon, a healthy food source, are facing extinction, almonds and pistachios are not."

Trinity and Klamath tribes ran and prayed with the Winnemem Wintu runners along the route that brings Trinity water into the Sacramento River and then down to industrial farms in the Central Valley.

As the Winnemem Wintu Tribe and other Sacramento River, Bay Delta, and Bay Area tribes ran, rode on horseback, boated, biked, and prayed for the salmon, a massive adult fish kill of ESA-listed spring run Chinook salmon unfolded on Butte Creek, a tributary of the Sacramento River.

Butte Creek was the one watershed in California where spring salmon were actually recovering. Over twenty thousand adult spring salmon were returning to Butte Creek to spawn when they began to die from the outbreak of two fish diseases, *ich* and *columnaris*. At least twelve thousand fish have died so far. Local advocates blamed Pacific Gas and Electric dams and diversions for the fish kill.

"We have to allow fish to swim into the upper watershed and make sure that the water is cold by not diverting it out of the stream. What a tragedy it is to lose so many fish when there's available habitat and available water and a failing PG&E hydroelectric system is the only thing in the way," Allen Harthorn of Friends of Butte Creek told Dan Bacher of the *Sacramento News and Review*.

In the Klamath watershed, the annual Salmon River spring salmon dive had even bleaker news. Less than two months after their listing under the California Endangered Species Act, only one hundred wild adult spring salmon, once the predominant run in the watershed, had returned.

"The cultural significance of the spring salmon is beyond Euro-American conception. It's more than just a policy trying to get passed through, or a biological opinion," said Ryan Reed, a member of the Hoopa Valley Tribe and Karuk spring salmon ceremonial priest. "The spring salmon are our relatives who are facing extinction, and a part of our lifestyle, cultural longevity, and the survival of my people."

Reed was one of many tribal members who testified at a state ESA hearing this spring that the last thing they wanted was for such an important food source to be listed as threatened, however extinction was a worse option.

Right after the Run4Salmon concluded with an intertribal ceremony just north of San Francisco, the California SWRCB made the decision to finally curtail additional Bay Delta farmers and closed public comment on curtailing irrigation deliveries on the Scott and Shasta Rivers.

Regina Chichizola from Save California Salmon testified in favor of the curtailments at a State Water Board hearing.

"These curtailments are vital and coming a little too late," said Chichizola. "We've let the fish die. Fishermen and tribes are facing incredibly huge losses over and over again."

Save California Salmon is one of several organizations asking for the state to reassess water rights in California. Chichizola explained in a letter to the editor in the *Los Angeles Times* in June: "Who gets clean water in California is a social justice issue. . . . The climate crisis highlights the fact that California has to reassess its antiquated water-rights system. Cities, Native people, and rivers should not continue to be without water while farmers flood their land."

THE WEST BERKELEY SHELLMOUND: A LEGAL BATTLE THAT HAS INSPIRED A GENERATION

MICHELLE L. LAPENA AND VIOLA LEBEAU

To be wealthy was not to have, to be wealthy was to give.
—Malcolm Margolin, The Ohlone Way

A cross the globe, Indigenous people fight for their cultural and ancestral livelihoods through the protection of sacred sites. These sites, often deemed insignificant by those who don't understand, are under significant threats from development, which further continues the history of cultural and ethnic genocide against Native people and their homelands. In the case of the West Berkeley Shellmound, the Lisjan people resided in the East Bay Area when

Bibliographic references for this essay can be found in the References and Notes section at the back of the book.

missionaries and colonists first came to Northern California, and despite a history of missionization, genocide, exposure to European disease, and forced cultural assimilation, they are still here and continue the battle to protect their ancestors.

We know from mission records that the first contact between Ohlone groups and the Spanish probably took place in 1602 when Sebastián Vizcaíno's expedition arrived in the Monterey area, searching for a safe harbor for Spanish ships. But it wasn't until 1769, when Gaspar de Portolá's expedition arrived in the Monterey area and established a presidio, that the Ohlone began to have continuous contact with the Spanish. "Contact" is a generous word. The mission system sought to destroy traditional Ohlone lifeways without any real attempt to understand them.

That the Ohlone people continue to live in their homelands is nothing short of a miracle, but survival came at great cost. When the Spanish missionaries first saw the lands of Huchiun, they saw an abundant land that supported many tribelets. They also saw in the Ohlone the opportunity to subjugate Natives for slave labor and to convert them into neophytes. But back then, and thereafter, it was the shellmounds that captured the interest of all who saw them.

A shellmound is a complex, cone-shaped structure built by Ohlone people over many thousands of centuries of use, until the Spanish missionaries arrived and began to colonize the Native lands. The Ohlone built the shellmounds out of the remains of the dead, which included the remains of Ohlone people as well as the remains of all other creatures and plants that they consumed. That the Ohlone buried their dead in mounds with the remains of abalone, clam, mussel, oyster, and cockle, as well as the bones of other mammals, has always confused non-Indians. A 1942 editorial by Hal Johnson for the *Berkeley Daily Gazette* provides the most common interpretation of a shellmound by non-Indians: "As you undoubtedly know, a shellmound was the combination *burial ground and garbage dump* of California's first settlers. Mounds grew as departed Indians were buried there in shells" (emphasis added).

The difficulty in the translation from the Ohlone perspective to the non-Indian perspective comes from the non-Indian perspective's separation between humans and the rest of the environment. The remains of all who lived before are considered sacred; whether it is a human or a clam, it is valuable. The shells of the clam, abalone, oyster, mussel, and cockle are so valuable to the Ohlone—in fact, to all California Indians—that they were (and still are) sanded, drilled, and lovingly crafted into fine jewelry. To be buried in the shells of these important sea creatures, even today, would be an incredible honor.

It is believed, based on maps from Spanish missionaries and others, that there were at least 425 shellmounds around the shores of San Francisco Bay and many hundreds more across the central California coast. The West Berkeley Shellmound, which is located just off the University Avenue exit from I-80, heading up the hill toward the UC Berkeley campus, is one of those shellmounds that has been under continued and direct threat ever since.

Located at the original shoreline and by the mouth of Strawberry Creek, the Shellmound is estimated to have been thirty feet high and one hundred yards long, a burial ground for ancestors of the Ohlone of the East Bay and a sacred place. Ohlone people inhabited a village adjacent to the Shellmound continuously from around 3,700 BC to 800 AD. At that point, the village was relocated nearby, but the mound had ongoing ceremonial purposes, including as a burial site. While white settlers removed aboveground portions of the mound for roads and other commercial purposes between the years of 1853 and 1910, the subterranean portions of the mound remain.

By 1902, the University of California at Berkeley had established its new anthropology department, which was the first department of anthropology in the western United States. The department's first focus was the excavation of Bay Area shellmounds. The West Berkeley Shellmound was identified as an "archaeological deposit" that represented the lifeways of the Ohlone people. Although there were still Ohlone people living in the Oakland area who could have helped the anthropologists gain insight into Ohlone ways, UC Berkeley archaeologists decided instead to excavate the mound to see what was inside. The West Berkeley Shellmound, like many others in the area, became a source of new wealth for UC Berkeley. The "collection" of ancestral human remains and artifacts from the West Berkeley Shellmound is still held by the Phoebe Hearst Museum and includes a large number of tools and ornaments as well as at least ninety-five Ohlone ancestors.

The Ohlone Village and Shellmounds site was landmarked by the City of Berkeley in 2000 (Wollenberg 2008). But the discovery of two sets of ancient human remains situated outside of the previously established boundaries of the Shellmound during more recent road construction at 1919 Fourth Street has prompted calls to update the borders of the Shellmound (Dinkelspiel 2016). To the naked eye, it is a 2.2-acre parking lot with development opportunity next to what used to be Spenger's Restaurant. To the Ohlone, the remains of the Shellmound call out to be restored. A group of Ohlone have answered this call and developed a plan to restore the Shellmound rather than destroy what is left.

Unfortunately, despite the presence of Native American human remains at the site, developers do not see its cultural value; Lauren Seaver, vice president of development for Blake Griggs Properties, stated "There is nothing at all of any cultural or historical significance on this property whatsoever" (Shellmound, n.d.). They believe that the land should be developed for commercial purposes, specifically a five-story retail-condo development. Ohlone tribal leaders are calling for the preservation and restoration of the lot as a historic site and natural area. Corrina Gould, spokesperson for the Ohlone

Confederated Villages of Lisjan, has led a five-year effort to create an inspiring memorial park that would daylight Strawberry Creek and include a memorial and educational cultural center. The tribe has worked with Sacramento Indian law attorney Michelle LaPena (Pit River/Maidu/Cahuilla) of the law firm Rosette, LLP, to make good faith offers to the landowners, but each offer to negotiate a purchase of the land to date has been rejected. As a result, the use and occupancy of the land has become a legal battleground that is now in the hands of the California courts.

———

LITIGATION FILED

After the original submission of the project to the City of Berkeley, which triggered AB 52—a law passed in 2014 that requires tribal consultation for any project subject to review under the California Environmental Quality Act (CEQA) that may impact a traditional tribal cultural resource—the project began to stall because of a failure to come to an agreement during the consultation. Subsequently, a new law, SB 35, was passed to streamline certain projects that might otherwise be covered by CEQA and AB 52. The developers amended their development application so that they could try to meet the lower standard of SB 35, but the city denied the streamlined application, in part because of the presence of the Shellmound on the site and because the project did not meet all the criteria set forth in SB 35.

In August 2018, West Berkeley Investors walked away from the project, but the owners of the lot, Ruegg & Ellsworth and the Frank Spenger Company, pushed forward with the development plan, suing the City of Berkeley in November 2018 for denying the SB 35 application. In answering the complaint, the city argued it had been allowed to deny the SB 35 application because of the parcel's landmark status. The Confederated Villages of Lisjan joined the city in the lawsuit. In the meantime, the city has approved two other

SB 35 affordable housing projects, on Oxford Street and Berkeley Way, projects that did not have significant impacts to tribal cultural resources and that otherwise met the criteria of SB 35 (Hicks 2019).

In October 2019, the Alameda County Superior Court ruled in favor of preserving the West Berkeley Shellmound. Judge Frank Roesch's ruling affirmed that the proposed development project at the West Berkeley Shellmound site did not meet the requirements for approval under SB 35. Importantly, Judge Roesch agreed with the Confederated Villages of Lisjan and the City of Berkeley that the West Berkeley Shellmound constitutes a historic structure, even though it has been demolished above ground. Under the terms of SB 35, a project is disqualified if the project site contains a historic structure. In his ruling, Judge Roesch wrote: "A historic structure does not cease to be a historic structure or capable of demolition because it is ruined or buried. That proviso is without basis in the text of the statute and would exclude many of the world's most beloved archeological treasures, such as Hezekiah's tunnel in Jerusalem, the Roman ruins in Pompeii, the mausoleum of Qin Shi Huang, the cave cities of Cappadocia, and the tombs in the Valley of the Kings. Any reading of a statute protecting historic structures that would exclude such features from protection must be rejected" (Shellmound 2019).

While the city and the tribe prevailed in the lower court, the private owners appealed the case to the California Court of Appeal. Complicating matters, in September of 2020, while the litigation was working its way through the courts, the California Legislature passed AB 168, which amended SB 35 to require tribal consultation for housing projects that would impact tribal cultural resources. The California Court of Appeal is now called on to decide whether that amendment has retroactive effect or if the original law alone calls for protection of the site from streamlined development.

As the authors were completing this writing in April 2021, the

Court of Appeal ruled against the city and the tribe, and overturned the favorable decision by the trial court. The Court of Appeal judges failed to understand the structural nature of the Shellmound and in fact went so far as to state: "There is no evidence in the record that the Shellmound is now present on the project site in a state that could reasonably be viewed as an existing structure, nor even remnants recognizable as part of a structure" (*Ruegg & Ellsworth et al.* 2021).

The failure of the court to appreciate the nature of the Shellmound really goes back to the quote by Hal Johnson, where he referred to the Shellmound as a garbage dump. Other language in the opinion reflected the same Eurocentric bias that the United Auburn Indian Community cautioned against in the amicus brief they filed in support of the city and the tribe. Sadly, the court was unable to overcome this bias and therefore failed to grasp the legal arguments that were made by the city and the tribe.

With a ruling like this, the city and the tribe must evaluate whether to appeal. If there is no appeal, the court has directed a remand back to the lower court to issue a writ of mandate ordering the city to approve the project application. While there are many technical issues to resolve with this litigation, appeal does seem likely. But as this case shows, the only way to truly protect the West Berkeley Shellmound is for the current owners to sell the land to Ohlone people to preserve and restore it.

———

NATIONAL TRUST FOR HISTORIC PRESERVATION

Because of the obvious historical and cultural significance of the West Berkeley Shellmound to the local Native people, as well as so many others from across the state, the country, and the world, the National Trust for Historic Preservation filed an amicus brief in the lawsuit. The trust argued that the West Berkeley Shellmound is an invaluable cultural resource worthy of preservation and should be protected by California state law. At the crux of this lawsuit are two legal questions that are relevant to the trust's priority concerns: Does an Ohlone shellmound qualify as a historic "structure" eligible for protection under SB 35? Will the Ohlone have a voice in the decision-making process?

"The National Trust's advocacy for the West Berkeley Shellmound and Village Site is motivated by our strong belief that the Ohlone tribe has the right to a say in what happens to a site that holds such deep cultural and spiritual significance to their community," said Katherine Malone-France, chief preservation officer of the National Trust for Historic Preservation. "In this instance, preservation is firmly on the side of equity and justice" (Shellmound 2020).

In addition to participating in the lawsuit as an intervening party, the National Trust for Historic Preservation also announced that they placed the West Berkeley Shellmound and Village Site on their 2020 list of America's Eleven Most Endangered Historic Places.

"We are incredibly honored and grateful to receive this recognition for the sacred site we have been fighting so hard to preserve," Corrina Gould of the Confederated Villages of Lisjan said. "Not only does it validate the historic significance of this site to the Ohlone people, but it also establishes one of our sites in its rightful place as a significant and essential part of the history of this region and the entire nation" (Shellmound 2020).

The trust has released an annual list of America's Eleven Most Endangered Historic Places since 1988, focusing attention on threatened one-of-a-kind treasures to galvanize the public to help save them. According to the trust, of the three hundred sites they have listed to date, 95 percent have ultimately been preserved.

———

HOPE FOR THE FUTURE

In addition to the support from the National Trust of Historic Preservation and the United Auburn Indian Community in the litigation, the West Berkeley Shellmound has attracted support from across the globe. From Berkeley to Mount Shasta, from Mauna Kea to Tibet, from Oak Flats to West Papua, and from the Amazon to Kashmir, the Shellmound has helped rally Indigenous communities from across the world in the fight against the destruction of sacred sites. Many of these supporters face similar battles in their own ancestral homelands and have dedicated their lives to protecting their own sacred sites from development and destruction. The leaders of the Run4Salmon journey from the McCloud River meet at the West Berkeley Shellmound each year, as a place of ceremony to begin their travels, and as Corrina Gould, spokesperson for the Confederated Villages of Lisjan and co-founder of Indian People Organizing for Change, has said herself, "It's not just for the Ohlone people, it's not just a ceremonial place where we pray, but a place the Bay Area in general can be proud of, as the oldest place people ever lived here. It's a wonder of the world, a place we should preserve."

The span of years between the arrival of Portolá and the attempted destruction of the West Berkeley Shellmound was a time when traditional Ohlone life was destroyed, but somehow Ohlone people survived, and so did the West Berkeley Shellmound. The most recent developments in California's court system have inspired a generation of Ohlone to stand up against continued destruction of their lifeways and culture. This effort is consistent with the Ohlone principle that "to be wealthy was not to have, to be wealthy was to give." Despite the advocacy efforts of Gould, the trust, and thousands of people across the globe, the work to preserve the West Berkeley Shellmound and Village Site is just beginning. One can hope that the vision of a restored West Berkeley Shellmound will someday become a reality.

EDUCATION

EDUCATION AS SELF-DETERMINATION

OLIVIA CHILCOTE AND CHRIS MEDELLIN

Native Americans and Western forms of education have a complicated history. During the nineteenth and twentieth centuries, the United States government facilitated a colonial project to assimilate Native Americans under the guise of education. According to a May 2022 report from the Assistant Secretary of Indian Affairs, the United States operated or supported 408 boarding schools across 37 states from 1819 to 1969. Twelve of these institutions were located in California. The infamous quote from the founder of the first off-reservation boarding school, Captain Richard Henry Pratt, "Kill the Indian in him, and save the man," encapsulated the intent behind boarding school policy. United States officials targeted Native American children in an attempt to "Americanize" and "civilize" them through a militaristic educational program that prohibited Native youth from speaking their languages or practicing their cultures. Native American children's forced enrollment at boarding schools ripped families and communities apart, disrupting traditional kinship patterns and cultural lifeways.

The boarding school system's legacy still impacts Native American communities and individuals as they grapple with chronic health issues, increased risk for depression and post-traumatic stress disorder, and intergenerational trauma.

In addition to the devastation wrought by boarding schools, many Native peoples remain wary of educational institutions like universities and museums that have a sordid history of appropriating and exploiting Indigenous knowledges and cultures. Uneven power relations between Native peoples and academic researchers, particularly from fields like archaeology and anthropology, historically played a role in the objectification, classification, and territorial dispossession of Native Americans. For example, the 1862 Morrill Act gave 148,686 acres of Ohlone land to the University of California to open its first campus in Berkeley, where anthropological researchers built successful careers documenting California Indian peoples and cultures. Stories of grave looters and museum collectors are still widely circulated among Native peoples as tribes continually struggle to repatriate ancestral remains and cultural objects from universities and museums.

Despite these histories and current struggles, we believe that Native people who obtain college degrees participate in acts of resistance and further tribal goals for self-determination. When Native students obtain degrees in fields tied to the subordination of Native American peoples, the power dynamic shifts. We, as Native peoples, can use educational attainment to tell our stories and write our own histories in the ways we want to be represented. We also believe that Native peoples need to be in charge of economic development, cultural resources, language revitalization, and resource management for their own and other tribal communities. Native students' engagement with higher education is a key to fully realizing tribal self-determination and the enactment of tribal sovereignty.

One of the ways in which educators can support marginalized students is to create programs that honor their cultural backgrounds and welcome them into spaces of learning. In 2013, a group of San Diego State University faculty, staff, and Native students alongside San Diego tribal community members developed Elymash Yuuchaap Indigenous Scholars and Leaders Program to ease the difficulties many Native American students experience in their transition to a large institution of higher learning. The late Larry Banegas of the Barona Band of Mission Indians gifted the name Elymash Yuuchaap, which is one way of saying "youth think" in the Kumeyaay language. All educators, regardless of their position at an institution, are responsible for understanding student barriers and challenges so they can work to eliminate real and perceived burdens. Shifting responsibility away from students and onto the university motivated administrators to approve the establishment of Elymash Yuuchaap, which fosters Native American student success. All incoming Native American students are automatically enrolled in Elymash Yuuchaap their first year on campus and attend the one-unit course every Friday afternoon. The Elymash Yuuchaap seminar course immerses students in various educational modalities that center Indigenous knowledge, identities, histories, languages, and cosmologies.

At the same time, the program assists Native students in building navigational capital, relationships with university officials, and specialized access to institutional resources. A structured peer mentoring component that pairs first-year and transfer students with Elymash Yuuchaap alumni provides another support system to new students as they build relationships grounded in the Native campus community. The intentional integration of Western ways of learning that complement and uplift Native American college students' cultural knowledge meets university strategic goals of inclusivity without requiring students to sacrifice aspects of their Native identity to earn a degree. Additionally, the goals of improving grade point averages, lowering stop-out rates and disqualification, and increasing the retention and graduation rates becomes an institutional burden to solve, with benefits that are determined by and for Native people. When asked what the Elymash Yuuchaap program meant to them, students indicated that it was a space to feel "at home," to foster a sense of safety and belonging, to create meaningful connections, and to succeed mentally, spiritually, and academically. Universities were not designed to center Indigenous students and Indigenous world views, but creating Native spaces in academic settings like Elymash Yuuchaap ultimately demonstrates that Native Americans can thrive on university campuses.

Pivotal to Elymash Yuuchaap's ongoing success is the program's integration with San Diego State University's Native Resource Center. The Native Resource Center was finally established in 2019 after decades of student activism. As Larry Banegas named Elymash Yuuchaap, honoring the local Kumeyaay community, Chairman Jon Christman of the Viejas Band of Kumeyaay Indians gave the Native Resource Center the name Wa Hahme, which roughly translates to "house of growth." The Native Resource Center uses culturally relevant research methods that serve tribal communities through the growth of every Native student who attends San Diego State University. The Native Resource Center provides an opening for Native students to reclaim their education in ways that respect their tribal communities, their complex identities, and their ancestors. Students are encouraged to participate in all aspects of shaping the Native Resource Center, from establishing the vision statements to producing artwork that is displayed in the physical space. Students direct the focus of upcoming events, lectures, workshops, and social justice initiatives that the Native Resource Center leads during the academic year. Utilizing a community-based/democratic approach, the Native Resource Center relies on input from student leaders, student assistants, faculty in American Indian studies and other departments, and center staff; all have a seat at the table in creating the support programs and services that empower Native students and facilitate their success. When a Native student walks into the center, they see themselves, their peers, and future generations of students welcomed to a new home on campus.

We encourage everyone to contact their local universities to find out if there are programs or events specifically for Native American students. Native-centered recruitment exposes youth to the possibilities of a university education that can inspire their career path and future. Visiting and eventually attending a college campus can be a meaningful experience to a young Native person and a pivotal step for increasing interest in higher education as an act of resistance to colonization and as a path towards tribal self-determination.

If you, your community, or any tribal youth are interested in learning more about Native American initiatives and programs at San Diego State University, please contact nrc@sdsu.edu.

CREATING CEREMONIES TO PROTECT US FROM TRAUMATIC RESEARCH

MAURA SULLIVAN

H ave you ever read something about your ancestors that left
you heartbroken? As our own people get more involved in
the scholarship of our tribal histories, we keep learning more about
aspects of colonization that add more to the story. For my tribe it is
the terrible destruction of our culture and way of life that the mission
system brought to California. When we engage with historically
traumatic material as Indigenous people, we have added layers
of complexity with the readings or research that our non-Native
colleagues do not experience. For many of us, college is the first time
we read about the genocidal tactics used against our ancestors. These
readings cannot be done in an afternoon and should not be taken
lightly. I propose that we look to our cultural practices and especially
our spiritual practices to guide us in this necessary but very painful

work. I have outlined a few ways to prepare to engage with traumatic material as well as what to do when you encounter it when you don't expect it. I also propose that racism within the university or in other places causes other traumatic experiences where we can use our cultural and heritage practices to protect ourselves.

This began for me as I was reading a book for class. I came across material about boarding schools. Although my family history does not include boarding schools, the trauma of reading about the experiences of Native youth and the attacks on their languages struck me deeply. I had to stop reading. I realized that this section was touching me on a level that my non-Native colleagues were not experiencing. At the same time a relative had sent me pictures of *kiynax'naxalamu'w* (our islands) and animals that live there. I also had pictures of family. This process made me realize that we should use pictures of our families and our homelands to disrupt the chaos of reading historically traumatic material. You will remember why you are doing this difficult work, it will give you spiritual sustenance to carry on. Taking a moment away from the reading and immersing yourself in a natural place if possible is also another strategy. But many of us are away from home and going to our ceremonial or sacred places isn't possible. Maybe you can find a place on campus that you like. Another strategy is to have someone from home send you pictures or videos of special places. When you are home from school take pictures of places and plants that are special to you.

These can all be part of your spiritual arsenal, a toolbox you can call on when you need it. Prepare for a reading with any spiritual protection that is special to you or your family. This could include the use of medicinal plants or objects. I have many shells and rocks from home that hold special power and medicine for me. Having these with you can help you during hard times. This could be done if you encounter a reading that you did not know would be harmful, or this can be done before a reading is started. Give yourself time and space to do hard readings.

I am especially inspired by the upcoming generation of scholars. No one ever told me about how to protect myself and ready my heart and mind for traumatic material. I hope aunties or uncles will read this article and think about the youths in their lives and be supportive of the work they are doing. I hope those youth will read this article and think about ways to protect themselves while engaging in the traumatic experience of higher education. These are learning experiences for you as a Native youth, these all make you a stronger person and a better scholar.

Some of the work I do regarding archives and historical narratives by white anthropologists puts me up against some of the most racist and vile characterizations about our people. It's hard to learn when you are in a very upset space—angry, sad, and disgusted. When you come up against that kind of material, stop, take a break, maybe journal about your experiences. Talk to other Native scholars doing this work. Write yourself a special prayer you say before you do hard readings. Write yourself a special song you can sing when you encounter hurtful content. If you can, look to your indigenous language to help you with these songs and prayers. These are all positive ways to process the violence of the past.

I am very grateful to have a chance to think about and write about this process that has developed for me recently. It is in engaging with my studies as well as engaging with my culture that I am finding balance. Being away from my family and from the California Indian community has been especially hard for me. But I am meeting Native people from the Gulf South as well as other Indigenous nations such as Maya communities from Guatemala. I want to be spiritually strong when I do this kind of nation-building work and especially when sharing the story about our experience with the mission system. Many people in the South have never heard our story. I hope this article will reach people who are doing hard work and that they can incorporate their own practices.

TEACHING ABOUT RACE IN A UNIVERSITY

ROSE SOZA WAR SOLDIER

Many California Indians share similar recollections of the notorious fourth grade mission unit. It is one of the few instances where California Indians are mentioned in K–12 curriculum and it overwhelmingly objectifies them.

Textbooks and lesson plans point out mission architecture, agriculture, and cattle. You learn about Serra, but not Toypurina. California Indians are firmly placed in the past, not the present. The fleeting mentions of California Indians in curriculum leads to a general public, and sometimes Indians, with a lack of knowledge of California's colonial history and Indigenous survival. When these students go off to college, they encounter histories and information that challenge their notions of California statehood, gold miner tenacity, and stereotypical imagery of Indians.

Universities are sites of knowledge and growth, and also sites of violent silence. California Indian art, baskets, recordings,

---

Bibliographic references for this essay can be found in the References and Notes section at the back of the book.

photographs, regalia, songs, and, most painfully, human remains collected by early anthropologists remain hidden and held in colonial archives and collections in California and across the country. Campus buildings are named for individuals who collected remains or celebrated "settlers." Some California Indian faculty experience isolation because they teach at campuses where they are the only Indigenous faculty. For many California Indians, teaching within institutions is an experience at times fraught with tensions largely unrecognized by the academy and colleagues. Simultaneously, teaching in higher education provides California Indian professors the opportunity to expose college students to historically accurate information, discuss the construct of race and its application to California Indians, and assign robust work by Indigenous scholars, writers, and artists.

Race is a social construct, but it impacts daily lived experiences. Sociologists describe racialization as the process by which the majority population assigns superficial characteristics, segregates, attributes qualities, and acts upon perceived inferiority of the constructed "other." The hundreds of thousands of people who flooded California after the discovery of gold brought their concepts of race and racism. The racialization of California Indians inextricably connects to colonization and statehood, which had devastating and deadly consequences. John Bidwell authored one of the first acts passed by the newly formed California legislative body, the 1850 Act for Government and Protection of the Indian, followed by an amendment in 1860. This benign-sounding law led to the murder, kidnapping, enslavement, and rape of California Indians. According to the *Marysville Daily Appeal* in 1861, young California Indian women were kidnapped to serve both the "purposes of labor and lust" and purchased "for fifty or sixty dollars for a young digger to cook and wait upon them, or a hundred dollars for a likely young girl." The racist slur "digger" appeared to apply primarily, though not exclusively, to central California, and was utilized to degrade and dehumanize California Indians as shorthand for uncivilized, uncultured, dirty, inferior, a group who consumed exclusively roots as a food source. An intentionally derisive slur, it diminished the diversity of tribal nations and placed California Indians as inherently less than human.

The racialization and dehumanization of California Indians led to a system of slavery and state-endorsed policies that supported genocide. State legislation, informally known as the Volunteer Act and Militia Act, supported voluntary militia groups who murdered thousands of California Indians in exchange for bounties. During his annual message to state legislators in 1851, the first civilian governor, Peter H. Burnett, stated, "That a war of extermination will continue to be waged between the races, until the Indian race becomes extinct, must be expected. While we cannot anticipate this result but with painful regret, the inevitable destiny of the race is beyond the power or wisdom of man to avert." In addition to referencing an Indian race, Governor Burnett also signaled the inevitable nature of extinction without referencing or reflecting upon his individual and government role in the systematic murders of California Indians. In contrast, a local newspaper commented on the rising bloodshed in the state. An 1862 *Daily Alta California* article noted that men "have for years made it their profession to capture and sell Indians, the price ranging from $30 to $150, according to quality." The article described men who do not hesitate "to murder in cold blood all the old ones, in order that they may safely possess themselves of all the offspring" to sell. Since the founding of the state, constructs of race, racialization, and racism have directly impacted California Indians.

Racial laws and policies central to the economic growth of the state largely disappeared from non-Indian public memory, replaced with stories of hardworking and virtuous individuals and families who single-handedly transformed the "wild frontier." Statewide,

California Indians could not attend public schools until the 1924 *Piper* decision and could not vote until the 1917 *Anderson* decision, and then only if they did not reside at a reservation. For nearly sixty years, beginning in 1854, it was a misdemeanor to sell guns or ammunition to California Indians under California Penal Code Section 398.

In addition to a racialized identity, Indians also maintain a political identity, as Native nations determine their citizenship criteria. The racial and political nature of California Indian identity is distinctive because for decades California Indians were not classified as citizens of the state, yet were required to abide by state laws. The eighteen unratified treaties negotiated in 1851 and 1852 resulted in a lack of a formal relationship with the federal government. As a result, for years California Indians were landless in our own traditional and historic homelands, and as non-citizens could not vote, testify in state court, or legally challenge slavery or abuse, and lacked the power to fundamentally protect families, children, and personal bodies.

Despite abundant records, many Californians are unfamiliar with this history of second-class citizenry. In addition to being a commentary on history and whose stories are valued and recorded, it further demonstrates the challenges of visibility for California Indians. This also connects to racialization, as many non-Indians hold a preconceived notion about the appearance of a "real Indian." In addition, Indians are placed firmly in the past and many non-Indians issue judgments of what qualifies one to be Indian, which usually includes a form of historical stasis. In a video on FNX First Nations Experience, Vince Medina (Chochenyo Ohlone) asserts, "just because you dress, you know, in a modern way, just because you like your, you know, iPad or whatever, doesn't mean you're not Indian." His comment confronts the issue of California Indians being judged inauthentic, often related to their being urban or contemporary, with non-Indians as the final arbitrator. Overwhelmingly, these beliefs held by non-Indians relate to caricatures, assumptions, and stereotypes. Many students embrace these ideologies, often perpetuated in popular culture, and carry them to college.

California Indian professors may experience student defensiveness around discussions of race and racialization. The Black/White binary paradigm dominates racial classification and politics through a myopic lens. Some students easily recognize racism, discrimination, and prejudice in the past but have difficulty recognizing it in its current structural and institutional forms or recognizing that racism and racist policies are not in the distant past. Indeed, professors' grandparents, great-grandparents, and great-great grandparents lived under these policies and all relatives lived, and continue to live, with racialization since contact with non-Indians. Many California Indian faculty experience having our perceptions of racial dynamics questioned, minimized, or denied. To assuage student resistance to historically accurate information, California Indian faculty navigate a number of different approaches in discussing race.

———

Dr. Don Hankins (Miwok) has taught Geography 106: The American West at Chico State for thirteen years and describes himself as "an anomaly," as he and one part-time lecturer in another department are the only Indigenous faculty on campus. A faculty member in the geography and planning department, he generally does not use the term "race" in his classes and instead uses "ethnicity" or "culture." He commented, "The challenge is to provide enough information to be interesting but not overbearing. On one occasion I had a student write on my evaluation of teaching that I should not cover so much on Native people." He continued, "My perspective is that this is one class out of their college experience which will provide exposure. The understanding of Native culture in this region is relevant to the way we live today as a broader society." The feedback from his student about too much information on Natives is commonly received by many California Indian faculty, particularly in classes that broadly approach race and ethnicity. All faculty need to review constructive course feedback, but they also need to contextualize comments that may actually highlight a student's discomfort with their first exposure to in-depth Indigenous histories and being asked to critically think about material. Generally, college is where many non-Indian students first learn about Native experiences in an in-depth manner.

Dr. Hankins further describes his approach to ethnicity within a greater context of equality versus justice. He details his process of "thinking of ecocultural equality, meaning our land and the life on that land is something we have kinship ties to, and it all needs to be respected. This point really gets at the intergenerational trauma and depression linked to environmental destruction and our connection to that." Part of this teaching approach includes getting students to recognize the power of place and role of purposeful cultural care, and how its lack results in environmental degradation and harm and cultural, mental, spiritual, and even physical trauma. This is explicitly tied to indigeneity, a significant difference between ethnic and Indigenous populations.

———

Dr. Melissa Leal (Esselen/Ohlone) teaches Introduction to Ethnic Studies and Ethnic Images in Film at Sierra Community College in Rocklin, which she describes as the "heart of gold rush" country. Similar to Dr. Hankins, she is the only Native faculty on campus and teaches Sierra's new Native American studies classes. She described her approach of introducing students to the local Indigenous community. For many Native faculty, one of the first imperatives is to ensure students' awareness of on whose land the campus resides. As Dr. Leal teaches a predominately non-Native student population, during the first few days of classes she assures her students that "no question is dumb and no question will go unanswered," and intentionally approaches classes through the prism of "we are all victims of racism and oppression—it just looks different in each of our groups." For a class exercise, she shares a photograph of a public lynching and asks students to identify the victim. Students easily identify the Black man lynched, but she points out the young white children present and asks her students to reflect on how this harmed them in a different violent manner. She believes that exposing students to accurate histories is about creating a space of mutual understanding for an informed student population.

———

Dr. Mark Minch-de Leon (Maidu) is an enrolled member of Susanville Indian Rancheria and teaches in the English department at the University of California, Riverside. The campus is unique in the state as there are twelve Native faculty on campus across different disciplines, the highest number at any UC. In discussing teaching, he stated, "The challenges come from an entrenched colonial education system and monopoly on reality." In speaking about the approach to the topic of Natives and race, he often begins "at conquest, with the debate that took place within the Spanish colonial administration over the in/humanity of Indigenous peoples, and tracks this through the colonial partitioning of forms of knowing that separated humans and nonhumans into distinct epistemological categories, thereby removing Indigenous relations to other than human beings, and therefore Indigenous worlds from political contestation and intelligibility." Through this approach, students are asked to consider the racialized dehumanization process and its implications as it relates to politics and the creation of knowledge in most academic fields, which were inherently dismissive of Indigenous people until relatively recently.

———

Shelbi Nahwilet Meissner (Luiseño/Cupeño) is a Ph.D. candidate in philosophy at Michigan State University. She has taught courses at the college level at both MSU and Saginaw Chippewa Tribal College, which primarily serves Anishinaabeg students, in Mount Pleasant, Michigan, where she is an adjunct professor of Native American studies. In her classes, she invites students "to problematize colonially imposed categories like race and gender" and unpack the "political status of being an enrolled member of a federally recognized tribe and cultural, spiritual, ethnic self-identity," which for Native students may have greater salience beyond an academic exercise, as it is a conversation about citizenship and family.

While at MSU, Meissner described being "newly acquainted with the racial politics of the Midwest" and the only Native woman TA for a general education philosophy class on race and ethnicity. She describes this class as "the most physically, emotionally, and spiritually draining semester" of her graduate career for a myriad of reasons, including attempts of physical intimidation by male students and a handful of student claims about her "obvious bias." The professor teaching the class provided unwavering support of her, yet one may wonder if a male non-Indian graduate student would have had similar experiences or would have automatically received respect from students. The perception of academic professionalism is racialized and gendered, as illustrated when Native women faculty are not accorded respect and it is assumed by students that what they teach is opinion rather than sociological data and objective, historically accurate information. Again, it is important for all professors to review student feedback, but it is equally important to contextualize it. Furthermore, any attempts at intimidation are fundamentally unacceptable and illustrate the intersectional experiences of a young Native woman in a relative position of authority in a college classroom. Meissner developed a class activity to help students gain a more insightful understanding of microaggressions. It includes five students reading aloud prepared scripts and a selected "main character" asked to guess the embodiment of the person based on observed microaggressions, then open it up to the class for discussion. Her experiences illustrate the range of college settings and the unique educational experiences at tribal colleges or universities (TCUs).

———

Leah Mata Fragua (*Yak tityu tityu* Northern Chumash) teaches Traditional Arts and Ecology and Anthropology of Northern America at the Institute of American Indian Arts in Santa Fe, New Mexico, a TCU. An adjunct faculty member in Indigenous liberal studies, her teaching approach centers an Indigenous worldview. Thus she teaches anthropology with a dramatically different lens than professors at a primarily White institution. She describes her expectations in class: "They will have to work hard. Research is a must as well as writing and public speaking. Many of our student population come from small rural schools, or are older adults who didn't have the privilege of going to college until later in life." She seeks to balance her rigorous expectations with some challenges: "Some of my students don't have access to Wi-Fi or running water when off campus. It challenges me to be creative in the classroom and find ways to address a student's needs so everyone has equal opportunity to succeed." She continues to state her unwavering support, understanding, and advocacy for students: "I am on the side of the student and while you have to work in my classes, I am aware of the diverse needs of our students and I work hard to meet those needs." While referencing the importance of assigning work by Indigenous authors, scholars, artists, and community members, Mata Fragua comments, "I believe as more Indigenous voices join academia, the more resources I can draw from, which adds strength to course goals and objectives. I also believe, as in anything in life, experience lets you build upon your work; it's a natural progression if you love what you are doing."

Many California Indian academics talk about history, textbooks, curriculum, and race within families and tribal communities in addition to classes. The number of California Indian faculty has been steadily growing for the past few years and we teach at universities, colleges, community colleges, and tribal colleges. Most enter the academy with an understanding of the numerous challenges and fully aware of the responsibility. California Indian faculty have a responsibility to all students but also serve as models and sometimes mentors for Native students. We are the Native voice in faculty meetings and meetings with administrators. We often serve on a number of committees as a diversity representative. We advocate for our tribal nations and for local tribal nations. This labor is not unique to California Indian faculty—indeed, most underrepresented faculty members finds themselves in this position. We understand this important work. However, in some instances colleagues and administrations lack understanding of this unseen labor.

California Indian faculty who experienced taking classes with Native faculty as undergraduate or graduate students point to that experience as a site of validation, more in-depth discussions, and seeing ourselves reflected and centered in class material for the first time. Some California Indian faculty experience challenges to our work or even our presence in spaces on university campuses. At times it is tedious teaching about race, particularly when students are overwhelmingly unfamiliar with Native histories and unique political statuses. However, to cultivate mutual understanding, students need to learn these important histories. Many California Indian faculty intentionally use historically accurate material to motivate and heal the wounds of the past for both Indians and non-Indians.

A WORD WITH CHIITAANIBAH JOHNSON

VINCENT MEDINA

The 2015 school year kicked off with big news: a young Maidu/ Navajo Sacramento State student named Chiitaanibah Johnson had challenged her history professor when he rejected the notion that what happened to Native people in North America was genocide. In reaction to her difference of opinion, he told her that she was expelled from his course.

When Indian Country Today Media Network first broke the story in September, droves of Native and non-Native people complained to Sac State via social media. People demanded answers as to why a Native American student would be denied the opportunity to voice her opinion.

Fortunately, Chiitaanibah ended up not being expelled and she is still speaking up about her convictions. Now, she is speaking to us. We had the privilege of talking with this valiant young woman about her ideas and aspirations and why she decided to speak out.

Chiitaanibah Johnson: [Introduces herself and her clan in her language.] My name is Chiitaanibah. I'm twenty years old. I go to Sacramento State. I'm an English major but I do a lot of dancing. I do a lot of acting. I love theater. I want to be a screenwriter and a playwright. I also want to pursue a degree in law. The goal would be to transfer to somewhere like Berkeley or Stanford and complete my B.A. there in government or political science with the theater and English minor, and then from there, hopefully transfer somewhere Ivy League for graduate school.

Vincent Medina: I see you have really big plans, that's great!

CJ: It's really exciting. I'm really interested in the government and how that works because I want to help people. The biggest dream I think I would have is to be a member of the Supreme Court but I would want to keep writing and acting and dancing.

VM: Wow. This just sounds really great. It's so wonderful that you have such big dreams for yourself and for your future. So, you've been in the news quite a bit lately. Can you describe what happened to those who might be unaware of the events at Sacramento State?

CJ: I was in a Monday/Wednesday/Friday class. And the professor was discussing Indigenous people, he said, "The genocide that took place," and then he paused and said, "You know. I don't like to use that word because it implies a purposeful decimation. Most Natives would be killed by European diseases and genocide insinuates that it was on purpose." The statement confused me. I didn't agree with it at all. There are so many Native people who were wiped out by European diseases but he didn't even mention the fact that those diseases were weaponized and very much purposely and maliciously sold and distributed in a mass amount of ways. He didn't say any of that and he just left it at that one statement. I went home. I hopped on my computer.

I did some research. I found some journals. I found some articles, including the United Nations definition of genocide. I highlighted it. I annotated it. I put a few references in there.

I put some documentaries that he could watch for himself and I brought that packet to class, because I knew that in that time and place, when he said that I was too mad—because it was like, "Alright. Here we are again in the classroom and we have a professor saying it wasn't genocide and you know, we're in college. I have a right to disagree in my way. I have a right to gather my own research and bring them forward and we can have a discussion. That was my mindset. It was . . . you know, this is the truth that's been so obscure, so hidden on purpose and I—because of the sacrifice of my ancestors made, I can sit here now and with the knowledge that I have, I can tell the truth. What happened in the class, he'd been talking about the European context for exploration, and he talked about the Portuguese being brave, ambitious men who'd made their wealth through trade. That was his lecture and he completely glossed over the African diaspora. He didn't mention any of their participation in that ugly, ugly slave trade.

At that point in the lecture, he was talking about a sailboat for fifteen minutes and I raised my hand. I said, "You know, I don't think that it's fair for you to talk about the Portuguese as if they were only brave and starving and ambitious. I'm sure that there were good men and I'm sure that they were brave and they were ambitious but the large majority of that history is covered in blood and the people that they conquered were not, did not just willingly give their lives and their culture and their country and their livelihood over to these people. It was genocide, it was murder." He says, "You don't have to start talking about the depopulation of the Americas yet." I said, "If you're teaching a truthful history class, yes you do, because this is how it transfers over."

Basically, the discussion's getting more heated and he says, "We're not going to talk about this." I said, "Why not?" It was his words, he had brought it to the class. Then I asked him again, he said, "Okay." "Since we're talking, I'd like to ask you to clarify the statement that you made on Wednesday in class. You said that you didn't like to use the word genocide. Why is that?" He said, "We're not going to talk about that." And he points at me. "We're not going to do that." I said, "Well, sir. You made this statement to the public. You made it to the classroom and that is a very heavy statement to make without any type of historical fact or proof or any academic findings of your own to support something like that, so why would you say it?" At that point, there was a student over here who turned around because I'd said, "The genocide that happened here was genocide. It was done on purpose. People were killed in mass amounts on purpose."

The kid turns around and he says, "No. That's not what he said. He said it was an accident." I just was like, "Do you see the difference between an Indigenous viewpoint and one that has been receiving the Eurocentric, whitewashed history over the course of many years until you get to the college era? And it's like you have so many opportunities to do this kind of research and find the truth. It's one Google search away. This is what oppression looks like. This is what the dynamic is between the people in power in our country and the people they committed genocide against." The teacher shut down class after I started reading from the United Nations definition because I had been talking and he said, "You know what? If you don't like it you can get out." I said, "Okay. I will, but before I leave, I can leave these packets of research here that I have done. They're fully annotated. Any of the students can read them, you can read them. It's got a lot of information in there about this topic, about the truth of this topic." He said, "It wasn't genocide."

I said, "Alright. United Nations definition of genocide is as follows." I started saying, "A. Intentionally killing members of the group, causing bodily harm to members of the group, inflicting physical . . . ." Then he stops me and he says, "Class, that's enough. Class is dismissed. I'm so sorry." Right in the middle of that, he stops the class, there were a couple of minutes left so he let them go a little bit early. He said, "I'm so sorry about this," like he was apologizing for my behavior and he said to me, he said, "I'm really starting to resent you being in my class. You've hijacked the last ten minutes of my lesson and we're done." This entire conversation lasted about five, seven minutes and he called me a hijacker. He said that I hijacked his—

VM: That's a loaded word right there.

CJ: That is a—and 9/11 was the very next week. It wasn't an accident. That's a very loaded word and after class, I went up to him and he kept saying, "I don't have time for this. I don't have time for this." I said, "These are your office hours right now, we do have time for this. What is it that you don't want to talk about?" He says, "You made me look like I was some kind of bigoted, prejudiced person. I'm trying to give a lecture about the Portuguese context for exploration. I do not appreciate that. Now I don't care what kind of scholarship you have, I don't care what your affiliation is with the university, I'm getting you out of here today and you are expelled from this class." When that happened, I didn't know that he can't do that. I just knew that here is a really angry teacher who was really upset with me. He's pointing his finger at my face. Even if it's just voice, he called me a hijacker when I presented my evidence, and I said, "I'm not doing—this isn't out of spite, this isn't out of malice. I'm coming from a place that's trying to tell the truth and I'm the only one here that wants to tell the truth." He said, "No. I don't think you are."

At that point, I said, "Look around you. We're the only two people left in this classroom. I'm the only person who's trying to tell the Indigenous side of history. I'm the only person in this classroom who cares and it's because I'm Indigenous." He said, "You know, I don't think you are. I don't think you are the only one." I said, "You're clearly not listening." He said to my argument—he points, he never picked up any of my articles, he never read them, he never listened to that side. He just shut it down because he didn't agree with it. He said, "This is a claim that people make, and I'm very familiar with these materials and if that's an opinion you have then we can talk about it after class." I said, "It's not an opinion. This is substantiated historical fact, and if you're going to make public statements that what happened to Native Americans wasn't genocide in an American history class, you better back it up."

At that point, he said, "We're not doing this. I'm done. I'm done." He left after promising to expel me from the course that day.

VM: What about the other students in class?

CJ: They were snickering off to the side and I heard a couple of people call me a crazy b***h off on the side and say, "She just wants attention," things like that off on the side. After—actually, when the teacher left, I could hear him outside with a student and his student said, "You know, professor. I'm so sorry. She's completely wrong."

VM: So nobody in the class that stood up for you?

CJ: No.

VM: That's just terrible too. That also makes me think how far we really have come that you could be in a university that's supposed to be full of learned people and nobody would stand up for justice. I think it says a lot about your own personal strength and conviction about this to tell the truth.

CJ: When it's a voice that they have tried to keep quiet since they landed in this country over five hundred years ago and that's the voice trying to tell us the message that we've been raised with and use it to fight that system. . . . It's no longer okay. It's no longer okay to stand up, it's no longer okay to have pride in yourself. It's no longer okay to fight for the truth because you are a hijacker.

VM: It's true. That's the thing too that I've noticed, especially since I've been in academia and all of that, it seems like most of society is comfortable with an Indian that weaves a basket or an Indian that does, that paints something or does a dance for them for presentation. When that Native person is asking and fights them with true scholarship on their same level, then all of a sudden you know, our voice doesn't matter as much to them. I feel like what we're doing today and what you're doing, what I see you doing—I don't want to put words in your mouth. It's like an extension of the things that our ancestors have done. Like our ancestors have always come up with very ingenious ways to fight back in different . . . you know, to fight for our land and our culture and our lives and our existence. We adapt to changes and we learn new tools to fight back with.

CJ: Exactly.

VM: As we're getting more and more sophisticated and educated in all this, this is just an extension of that. That's why I see this, so I'm sure. . . . Yeah, I'm sure your ancestors are proud of you too.

CJ: Thank you. What I'm really hoping is, like you're saying, media can be a friend. There's a lot . . . I can't help but notice parallels, the African American community has the Black Lives Matter movement. There's that movement but then because of that one hashtag, all these different people, all these different marginalized people with all their experiences, are voicing their stories and are demanding change. It's a slow process and, I mean, you can't just sit there and tweet about it. It's part of it. It's coming together in that that sense of unity and us, as Native people, we can find each other easier with these technologies.

VM: Social media and all of that.

CJ: Yeah, and things like changing the curriculum. It's been so hard to do in the past because it's only been, not like a small group of people, but in the face of the entire United States of America. It's only a small amount of people fighting for it. If we have platforms such as this to say, if we really want to change it, we really can do it, but it comes from every single person who takes time to really think this is it. This is why I was born at this time, this is why I've had the experiences I've had, this is what I've been, without knowing it, this is what I've been in a sense preparing for, and it's so that we as a nation, we as all are different nations, the first nations coming together and saying, "We're not going to take this anymore." And we have the chance to say, "We want the curriculum changed."

We want to be included. Our voices matter. Our lives matter. Our students matter. Our history matters. The more people that you get saying that and the more people that you get refusing to back down and give up, the more change that you are going to create. It takes time and it takes patience. We've been patiently waiting for so long and it's like now is the time. Now is the time to spring off of that. It's like it's easier to pull the trigger and say, "Alright, I'm going to stand up and do it," when you think about all the sacrifices and miracles it took just to be an Indigenous person alive. Period.

The fact that this, since the first time or first contact and all the horrible, really devastating and traumatizing atrocities—ever since that happened, there's been this trickle, and out of all the survivors, you made it here. It's not fair. It's not right, but you have a duty and you have a responsibility to fight the way they fought because now you're here. Good Lord, that is a miracle in itself and we can do it now. We can do it because they're not openly lynching people anymore. They're not openly shooting people. We don't have a bounty on us anymore. We can vote. We have our own phones. We have our own voices. We've got access to books. We've got access to all these different things and all it takes is the decision that we want to continue.

VM: You're right.

CJ: [Speaking to her father] Your great-grandfather fought the entire World War I, came back with an honorable discharge, and had to wait three years before he could vote.

VM: That is just injustice.

CJ: See, with that injustice, how could I possibly sit in a classroom that tells me genocide isn't what happened? While we still have people on reservations without clean water, without adequate heat; as long as we have elders who aren't receiving the proper shelter in the winter time or the summer time; as long as we have women, and men too, who have been unknowingly and forcibly sterilized; as long as we have history books that are still perpetuating the erasure of our history, we are going to have people like me and like you and like my dad, and people like this, everywhere. As long as that oppression exists, they are going to have resistance.

MY UNIVERSITY, MY ANCESTORS

EMILY CLARKE

I walk onto my college campus, where large grayscale buildings and concrete sidewalks suffocate the traditional lands of my people. Perfectly manicured lawns cover the earth that was once tended to by my ancestors. I imagine mesquite trees scattered across campus, shedding golden pods each summer. Perhaps there was deergrass growing where the dining hall now stands. I have always been the type of person who keeps observations like this to myself—little secrets I use like painkillers when academia throws its sticks and stones. There is a purple dragonfly on the bush next to my classroom. The girl outside the best on-campus coffee shop is wearing beaded earrings. Someone stuck a Land Back sticker onto the bicycle rack. These are the small signs that we are here. These are the moments that guide me into each lecture.

On the first day of school, I suffer through icebreakers in every class period. At this point, I haven't yet learned that it is easier, less emotionally taxing, to give my peers a rough estimate of where I am from rather than saying *I'm from the Cahuilla Reservation*. Each time I say the word "reservation," my icebreaker partner's face becomes a blank wall. *Wait, so you're like, Indian?* one says. *I thought you guys were all like . . . you know, dead.* I sit in a room full of students who are unaware of the possibility of my existence. Each professor, a painful grin plastered onto their face, encourages us to make friends with the person sitting next to us. *Hi, my name is Emily. Hi, my name is Emily. Hi, my name is Emily and I'm from the Cahuilla Reservation. Hi, my name is Indian. Hi, my name is Dead. Hi, my name is Artifact. Hi, my name is Myth. Hi, my name is Emily. What's yours?*

My university releases a land acknowledgement and reads it before every event. Plasters it across the website. Calls themselves progressive, woke, willing to practice reformation. Now, each student knows whose land they're on. Cahuilla, Tongva, Luiseño, Serrano. Somehow, knowing this makes me feel worse. Now, they can't use ignorance as an excuse. Now I can't use their ignorance as my excuse to forgive them. Land acknowledgements are the new trend for colleges across the country. Academia is White and guilty, so it self-soothes by writing a paragraph about the genocide of my people. But even I, the writing major, know how weak words can be. What is acknowledgment without action? What is forgiveness without apology?

My university begins a series of Cahuilla language courses and allows students to take the classes in order to fulfill their "foreign" language requirement. In a classroom full of students learning my traditional language, I am still the outsider. Imposter syndrome sits next to me in a plastic chair, whispers—*That white boy learned his vocab faster than you. His accent is better.* Imposter syndrome writes its name next to mine on my homework, leaves a note asking—*Shouldn't you already know all this?* Friends ask me for help studying for quizzes on verbs and pronouns. I can't tell them that I mixed up the difference between "she" and "they" on the last quiz. Admitting to this would strip me of any authenticity I have left. I would be without horse, without bow and arrow, without war paint and basket hat. And who am I if not the token Indian? What is my purpose if not to fulfill my university's idea of diversity?

My university pretends they don't know what the Pretendian list is. One of their diversity hires, a woman teaching Native studies in the ethnic studies department, turns out to be a fraud. She claims Cherokee, and has for years, even after being exposed multiple times. The *New York Times* releases an article about her deception and my university hunkers down like an animal during winter. There seem to be a pair of lips, shushing frantically, around each corner of the ethnic studies building. The woman has written books on Missing and Murdered Indigenous Women, she has taught classes about the role of women in tribal communities, she has pretended to be one of us while profiting off of our experience, our loss. I am seething every day, yet still I shrink. My university hides her away like a family heirloom. I imagine her sitting in her home office, surrounded by framed awards for her tireless work to give Native women a voice. I imagine her voice coming out of my mouth, demanding something be done. Maybe academia would listen then.

I find space to breathe in my Native studies classes. There are other Native students scattered throughout the classroom, grouped together like birds in the back of each lecture. We have grown up learning our history from elders, from stories passed down through generations, from tribal members gathered around a fire. Now, we read about it from hundred-dollar textbooks. We get quizzed on history that lives inside our bones. Our ancestors watch us, fill our notebooks with invisible prayers. Their hands, warm and soft, reach up from beneath the land to guide us towards another lecture hall, study group, research trip. Higher education was not meant for us, yet we are here. We exist in multiple worlds. Some of us live on our reservations and spend weekends cooking traditional foods for gatherings. Others drive to campus from the city, our car speakers splintering with the crashing sound of gourd rattles like ocean waves. We are gatherers, dancers, scholars, the descendants of a people stronger than the woven fibers of a yucca plant. We are here, we are here, we are here.

The girl in my fiction class writes a story about the boarding schools. "I learned about them in my history lecture," she says, "and I just felt so bad for the Indians." We are not the only ones that academia has given the opportunity to learn our history. Non-Natives major in Native studies, learn more about us than we sometimes know about ourselves, build an entire career out of our suffering. How weird it is to hear fairytales of my pain from the mouths of others. The girl reads her story aloud, pausing for dramatic effect after each mention of feathers in the hair or tipi smoke while I scribble lines of poetry onto a scrap piece of paper. *This campus is nothing like a home. Nothing like men holding shovels at a funeral or the clouds of dust their brown bodies create as soon as the priest says amen. Educated and Indian, I become one of the owls that spill broken spoken word from their beaks outside my reservation window. Academics tell me historical trauma lives in my DNA, as if I couldn't already feel it digging holes in my body. I am not the Indian you wish I was. This morning on the way to campus, I stopped my car to stare at Coyote dead on the side of the road, his mouth open as if to sing. My people were there with us, I felt their presence like heat radiating from the asphalt. My people are here now. They stand behind me, pushing me forward with palms firm as mortar stones.*

SOLIDARITY

CALIFORNIA INDIANS AND CALIFORNIA LOVE: BELONGING, KINSHIP, AND LAND

ROSE SOZA WAR SOLDIER

Tribal identity formation in the United States is nuanced and influenced by colonial definitions. Tribal definitions vary across tribal nations but are dramatically different than self-identification. Karuk writer and poet Julian Lang offers a succinct definition: "Wherever we go, we are known by someone there. Wherever we go, we discover that we know someone there" (Lang 2002, 113). In describing embedded social networks based on kinship, his comment illustrates that you know who you are and are known by the community.

There are many aspects to being Indigenous, with connection to land a central tenet. The concept of homeland for Indigenous peoples differs dramatically from many non-Indigenous people who may view land through the lens of property or resources rather than the origination of the people. In *Real Indians* (2003), Eva Garroutte

Bibliographic references for this essay can be found in the References and Notes section at the back of the book.

(Cherokee) outlines the varying manner of identity: legal, cultural, biological (primarily blood quantum), genealogy, and lastly self-identification. Self-identification is difficult as it includes people who may not know any specific tribal identity beyond family lore, which, while powerful, may or may not necessarily prove accurate. Kim TallBear (Sisseton Wahpeton Oyate) discusses Indigenous identity and DNA in her book *Native American DNA* (2013) and notes, "the story of tribal citizenship in the twentieth and twenty-first centuries is one in which dominant cultural notions of race—federal 'Indian blood'—have pushed and been pushed against by tribal peoples' own ideas of belonging and citizenship" (63). In several of my classes, students share with me that their great-grandmother was Indian of some ambiguous extraction.

Indians generally have a healthy skepticism of a self-identified Indian, particularly if there are no cultural or family connections—meaning we as Indigenous people want to know, who is your family? Who claims you? To be clear, self-identification is different than people and families who are known in the community but not enrolled in a federally recognized tribe. During the 1950s, the federal government policy of termination overwhelmingly targeted California, where over forty tribal nations were terminated, meaning their federal trust status ended and they were no longer eligible for rights including health care or trust lands. While several tribal nations worked through the court system, sometimes for decades, to have their federal recognition restored, there are still many California Indians who are recognized by the community but remain federally unrecognized.

An Indigenous identity is inherently political. In addition to the parameters for citizenship outlined by each tribal nation, many facets of tribal life require federal government approval, a residual from the US government's paternalistic position. Even the term used in North America to describe the Indigenous population (not including Native Hawaiians or Alaskan Natives) is debated. There are numerous terms that people, including myself, may use interchangeably: American Indian, Indian, Native, Native American, Indigenous, First Nation, Aboriginal, and, of course, our own tribal nations' names. In addition, common regional terms are California Indian and, more recently, California Native.

As a result of California's unique history, there are a significant number of federally unrecognized tribes and individuals who have fought for years to regain federal recognition. A California Indian identity emerged out of shared histories, common cultural markers, collective experiences of state and federal government policies, and a need to distinguish between those indigenous to the lands of what is now California and Indians who are not indigenous to the lands but reside in the state. Historic and contemporary intermarriage and relationships among California Indians, largely due to the relatively small populations and cultural taboo of marrying someone too closely related to your clan or family, contribute to a shared California Indian identity and multitribal people with extended families of different tribal identities. It is not uncommon to have California Indian families related to numerous tribal nations through marriage and children. In addition, as Deborah Miranda (Esselen/Chumash) notes in her book *Bad Indians* (2013), survival included marrying and bearing children with non-California Indians too: "By force, by choice, or by love, mixed-race unions were a tradition for those who survived the California missions" (xiv). Prior to contact and statehood, a broad California Indian identity did not exist. However, in the contemporary environment a California Indian identity exists and flourishes.

When declaring a California Indian identity, we are asserting humanity, personhood, and belonging in spaces that are often claimed by non-Indians. Māori scholar Linda Tuhiwai Smith asserts that the ability to consider Indigenous people as not fully human or human at all illustrates "systematic fragmentation," leading colonized people to name and define our humanity because there is an "understanding of what it has meant to be considered not fully human, to be savage" (Smith 1999, 26). Building on earlier work, Tom Holm (2003) defines personhood as four "interwoven and dependent" factors: language, sacred history, religion, and land. An Indigenous California Indian identity is tied to lands, stories, and the declaration of our survival and humanity. In centering a California identity, we are basing it on our definition of California. There are major distinctions between stories about California and California Indian stories.

In the public imagination, California commonly appears as a mythic land of wealth, salvation, and idealism. It provided opportunities for new arrivals to gain quick wealth or re-make themselves. Popular culture is filled with references to an imagined California. In the musical landscape, songs like The Mamas & the Papas' "California Dreamin'," LL Cool J's "Going Back to Cali," Tupac's "California Love," and Biggie's "Going Back to Cali" describe images filled with sunshine and parties, leading to a yearning to be in the state. Led Zeppelin's "Going to California" is a song about a heartbroken man in search of a new start and love. Additionally, there are songs that reference the ideal beauty of bikini-clad female bodies (most likely conceived as white) in the Beach Boys' "California Girls" and Katy Perry's "California Gurls"; the video for the latter is filled with sugary confections. To be clear, those of us who came of age during the 1990s can be a proud California Indian and turn up "California Love" any time it comes on the radio. But the imagined California does not reflect California Indians, as we are consistently absent in the mythical land of opportunity. California Indians survived the history of the state and are fully aware it viewed us as obstacles to its progress. These songs highlight an imagined California in which there is no space for Indigenous populations. When we use the term "California," we are not referring to popular culture images.

"California Indian" is a short-hand term for recognizing family, remembering history, positioning ourselves within the land, and distinguishing ourselves. The insistence on our presence connects to recognition based on our definition, not someone else's. When introducing yourself to non-Indians, it is common to respond to inquiries that you are California Indian and then specifically reference your tribal nations or reservation/rancheria. Some may believe that by asserting a California Indian identity, individuals are subscribing and embracing a pan-Indian identity. A mono-lithic, one-dimensional Indian. In my experience, this is incorrect. No California Indian is rejecting, dismissing, or diminishing our tribal identities and families. Nor are we commenting on status in a federally recognized tribe. Instead, we are centering a place name for us. California. Our stories and place of California are drastically different from popular culture images. By initially naming yourself a California Indian, you are guiding a person to our identity and our place and remembering our past. This is particularly helpful for those outside of the state who are unlikely to be familiar with the names and lands of, for example, Cahuilla, Maidu, Pomo, Tolowa, Yokuts, or Washoe, among many others. Furthermore, for multi-tribal individuals and families, it is a way to embrace your complete self and tell your story.

Rupert Costo (Cahuilla), president of the California-based American Indian Historical Society, often spoke out against a pan-Indian identity. He called it "historic extermination" and cautioned that a pan-Indian identity must be rejected because of the danger it posed to tribal cultures. He stated, "I am afraid this kind of unity which is based on smoothing out cultural differences will destroy us quicker than the efforts at assimilation have done so far" (Costo 1977, 33).

He spoke about rejecting pan-Indian identities, even though that may be difficult for the uninformed Indian and non-Indians. Never one to be circumspect with his words, Costo asserted, "it is too damn bad. A little bit of time and trouble will straighten them out." He continued, "we will not give up our tribal customs, or attire, or traditions, or ceremonial dress, just to make the Indian more appetizing to the so-called Pan Indian movement" (Costo 1977, 34). Costo clearly defends the importance of maintaining tribal cultures; however, as the president of a multi-tribal organization, he also recognized the significance of building coalitions and alliances between and among tribal nations and tribal peoples. A California Indian identity maintains a tribal identity and recognizes our connections.

As a graduate student at Arizona State University, I was excited to be on a college campus with a relatively large Indian student, faculty, and staff population. However, I also encountered a handful of Indians who told me to my face that they thought all California Indians died a long time ago. I missed home and California Indians. On the first day of a new semester, I took a seat in my Indian Education 530 class: Issues in Language and Literacy of Indigenous Peoples. In a small seminar class, I sat next to a woman wearing abalone. Dr. Kathryn Manuelito (Diné) had us introduce ourselves to our neighbor. To my surprise and excitement, I learned the graduate student I sat next to was Kishan Lara (Hupa/Yurok). We quickly spoke in hushed tones beyond any superficial initial introduction to learn about mutual connections, family, friends, and places. Though not directly related, we determined a distant cousin of mine from Soboba married someone from Hoopa. It was validating to speak with someone who knew the places and people I spoke about and vice versa. As Julian Lang described, we were known, and knew each other, lands, and families.

This experience illustrates the connection we had with each other, hundreds of miles away from our homes. From that point on, we were best friends in graduate school despite being in different departments; she was in education and I was in history. At conferences when Dakota and Lakota colleagues teased her about eating salmon, together we teased them back. We still joke about how only two California Indian graduate students would find ourselves in the same class and accidentally on purpose, since I noticed her abalone jewelry, sit next to each other on a campus with over seventy thousand students. Two California Indian women made it through graduate school outside of the state, in part because we supported each other.

Historian William Bauer (Wailacki and Concow) describes in his book *California through Native Eyes: Reclaiming History* (2016) that early California Acts defined a broad California Indian identity. He notes, "The California Jurisdiction Act defined 'Indians of California' as 'all Indians who were residing in the state of California on June 1, 1852, and their descendants living on May 18, 1928.'" This resulted in a compromised Indigenous identity that ignored tribal nations' sovereignty and political systems and treated everyone the same because the US government made no distinctions. He continues that, "By creating a racialized and homogenized identity of 'Indians of California,' the claims case was one of many assimilation policies" (25). Early federal and state policies overwhelmingly treated California Indians identically through racialization. State and federal government officials infrequently dealt directly with tribal nations in California. Spanish and Mexican systems provided limited opportunity to become *gente de razón*, while the US system regarded California Indians as inherently incapable of humanity, with cultures disregarded as inherently and immediately inferior. In the aftermath of state genocide and unratified treaties, the US government moved to more subtle forms of attack to erase us on paper with the introduction of blood quantum requirements and enrollment in federally recognized tribes.

This imposed colonial system limits enrollment to one federally recognized tribe. A significant number of California Indians are multi-tribal and many California tribal nations utilize direct descent genealogy for citizenship purposes. However, someone may not be eligible for citizenship if a tribal nation chooses to use blood quantum and an individual is below the threshold. As a result, a common conversation many Indians have when seriously dating is where any children they might have would be enrolled. Generally, our parents choose where we will be enrolled for citizenship. Despite the purposeful limitations of a colonial system of enrollment, it is possible to maintain connections to different tribal nations and consider multiple places home. I am not less of a Mountain Maidu woman because I am also Cahuilla/Luiseño and enrolled at Soboba. My family and I are known at both Susanville and Soboba.

Recently, stories of disenrollment (formal removal from tribal citizenship rolls at tribal discretion) at a number of California tribal nations received media attention. Generally, media outlets frame disenrollment as solely an issue of greed as tribal nations with gaming want to shrink their populations to ensure larger per capita payments. In part, reporting in this manner invites the public to issue condemnations and seize upon the idea that Indians engage in unscrupulous behavior like any other American, and by extension question the reason Indians have gaming. Furthermore, the reporting lacks the nuance to understand that tribal nations hold a fundamental right to determine their citizenship criteria. Unfortunately, news stories offer a reductionist interpretation without historical contextualization. Additionally, most news stories overlook Graton Rancheria's decision to formally introduce constitutional language banning disenrollment.

Historically, blood quantum never determined one's belonging. Rather, a collection of cultural and kinship aspects made us belong. Perhaps most central was land. Not ownership of it, but belonging to it. We are Indigenous because of our relationship with and belonging to ancestral lands. As Miranda comments, "Who we are is where we are from. Where we are from is who we are" (194). The central social and cultural tribal nation formation is land. The land anchors one's identity and even if one lives in a city or outside the state, you can always go home. Furthermore, sometimes cities are located within historical territories and being a city resident does not make one less of an Indian.

By naming and claiming a California Indian identity, we are simultaneously naming our place and building solidarity between different tribal nations in the state and within Indian Country. We recognize the California Indian population is relatively small and individual California tribal nations' populations are even smaller. To achieve our goals, it is necessary to coordinate and work as a larger collective constituency. In addition, one does not need to be a citizen of a particular tribal nation to recognize the importance of an issue and offer support. This can be observed outside of the state with support for the Dakota Access Pipeline protest: a number of California tribal nations sent supplies and several California Indians traveled there to offer support. California tribal nations' flags were raised and flew over Flag Road. In addition, tribal nations engage with and support issues and concerns around the state. A common example most people would recognize is gaming, through the successful ballot initiatives Proposition 5 and Proposition 1A. Tribal nations also coordinate around issues involving sacred sites, water rights, fishing rights, burial ground sites, environmental racism, land contamination, and others. California Indians engage with our traditions, memories, practices, stories, and histories. We acknowledge colonization yet recognize our identities are more than colonization. We survived under Spanish, Mexican, and finally American rule.

The unique history of California led to a racialization of California Indians wherein early writings discussed skin color and a perceived general ugliness, dirtiness, and animal-like nature. Early American arrivals "othered" California Indians and, by focusing on phenotype, argued that they were almost a different category of human in order to rationalize American treatment and oppression.

As a result, to proclaim a California Indian identity is to reject and challenge these racist characterizations.

The racist slur "digger" appeared in numerous publications and served to apply primarily, though not exclusively, to central California, and was utilized to degrade and dehumanize California Indians as an "uncivilized," "uncultured," "dirty," "inferior" group who consumed exclusively roots as a food source. An intentionally derisive slur, it diminished the diversity of tribal nations and defined California Indians as animal-like. In *Golden Dreams and Leaden Realities* (1853), George Payson contemptuously described California Indians: "monstrous heads, covered with a thick thatch of long black hair, and mounted on dwarfish bodies and distorted limbs, gave them a peculiarly inhuman and impish aspect" (256). In *The Land of Gold* (1855), Hinton Rowan Helper characterized California Indians as "Of all the aborigines . . . certainly the most filthy and abominable," and continued, "A worse set of vagabonds cannot be found bearing the human form" (268). He further dehumanized California Indians by describing them as "hungry wolves," waiting around for food from kitchens and slaughterhouses. Hubert Howe Bancroft wrote of California Indians in *The Native Races* (1886), "Their complexion is much darker to that of the tribes further north, often being nearly black, so that with their matted, bushy hair which is frequently cut short, they present a very uncouth appearance" (364).

These early characterizations by white Americans reveal how non-Indians categorized and classified California Indians. These publications undoubtedly impacted how non-Indians perceived California Indians and are only a small representation of the writings that can be found. The process of naming and claiming our identity along with our humanity and personhood is significant in combating a one-dimensional image largely informed by popular culture.

Many non-Indians hold a preconceived notion about the appearance of a "real Indian." California Indians are placed firmly in the past and many non-Indians judge what qualifies one to be Indian, usually based on a form of historical stasis. Indeed, we are often dismissed as extinct, sometimes even by other Indians outside of California. As I have noted in other essays, California Indians are judged as inauthentic, often related to being urban or contemporary, with non-Indians as the final arbitrator.

Overwhelmingly, these beliefs held by non-Indians relate to caricatures, assumptions, and stereotypes. Many non-Indians embrace these ideologies, often perpetuated in popular culture. Many non-Indians subscribe to this belief because California Indians do not resemble Indians in western movies. Perhaps the genre is best known for *Dances with Wolves* (1990) and *Last of the Mohicans* (1992). California Indians do not live in teepees, use drums (we use clapper sticks or gourds), innately know how to ride a horse (I learned as a child in Girl Scouts), and despite imagery in film, flute music does not randomly follow us. These are examples of how movies influence non-Indian expectations of a "real Indian." Most popular culture does not reflect California Indian peoples or cultures.

Of course, one must be careful not to generalize too much about a California Indian identity. Although a shared identity has emerged, cultural differences exist and tribal nations tend to have more cultural similarities with regional neighbors. Several state-wide organizations base membership on a California Indian identity: California Association of Tribal Governments, California Indian Conference, California Indian Legal Services, Intertribal Council of California—and this publication, *News from Native California*—all address the interests of California Indians. However, within state-wide organizations there are regional groupings; for example, the California Indian Basketweavers Association has groups for Northern California and Southern California. "California Indian" remains an inclusive term of tribal nation members indigenous to California, regardless of federal recognition or multi-tribal heritage. "California Indian" is our way of claiming our personhood and humanity,

BLACK LIVES MATTER ON INDIGENOUS LAND: SOLIDARITY IN SACRAMENTO

VANESSA ESQUIVIDO, MAYA ESQUIVIDO, AND MORNING STAR GALI

The year 2020 has no doubt been one of the hardest, as the world endures a global pandemic and Black, Indigenous, and People of Color (BIPOC) fight for liberation. Since the public lynching of George Floyd on May 25, 2020, and of several others, including Breonna Taylor, Ahmaud Arbery, and Tony McDade, a vibration has rippled throughout the world in protest. In this time of social unrest, California Indian communities are standing in solidarity with the Movement for Black Lives (M4BL) in Sacramento and beyond. We as a nation witnessed the outcries of historical injustices that continually target BIPOC communities. For example, people

---

This essay was published in the fall of 2020, shortly after the events recounted took place. Bibliographic references for this essay can be found in the References and Notes section at the back of the book.

KNOW WE ARE HERE

in Sacramento are calling for the Sacramento Police Department (SacPD) to be held accountable for the death of numerous Black individuals, including the highly publicized murder of Stephon Clark, whose life was stolen in the backyard of his grandparents' South Sacramento home in 2018.

Sacramento is in the traditional homelands of the Miwok, Maidu, and Nisenan peoples. It is also a place of immense activism, including this year's protests, centralized at Cesar Chavez Park in downtown Sacramento. Organizations leading the way and mobilizing include the Movement for Black Lives and Black Lives Matter Sacramento, Sacramento LGBT Center, Anti Police-Terror Project Sacramento (APTP), Showing Up for Racial Justice Sacramento (SURJ-S), and countless others, including many generations and decades of local Native organizing efforts. Through this article we want to recognize the labor of and momentum created by the global movement for Black lives. Indigenous peoples continue to benefit from the BLM movement, and we are not erasing generations of Native activism and work. We are finally seeing movement on issues that have remained stagnant for years, such as the removal of colonial statues, the name change of a racist football team, and reignited conversations around place names. Addressing the antiblackness within our own Native communities is work we still need to do. Accepting and hearing our Black Indigenous relatives' experience of racism within our own families is how we can start having those conversations.

———

BRIEF SACRAMENTO HISTORY

Growing up, we often learn about settlers as "heroes," their names splattered across our cities, freeway exits, and hospitals, becoming a part of our everyday lives. Sacramento is no different.

Learning the ahistorical account of John A. Sutter as a "founder" of present-day Sacramento silences the truth of the Miwok, Maidu, and Nisenan peoples by erasing their epistemologies and place names for this valley. Sutter's Fort, still standing in downtown Sacramento, is a continued memorialization of white settlers and a site of significant historical trauma for our Native community. Sutter's horrific accounts of enslavement of and violent attacks on our Native ancestors are conveniently left out as a part of settlers' moves to innocence (Tuck and Yang 2012).

It has been over a year since June 18, 2019, when California Governor Gavin Newsom apologized for the state-sanctioned genocide of California Indian peoples. This was a stunning difference from the first governor of California in the 1850s, Peter Burnett, who called for a "war of extermination [that] will continue between the two races until the Indian race becomes extinct" (Lindsay 2012, 231). Meaningful apologies need to have action behind them. The Sacramento Native community purposely held the De-Columbus event one year later, on the anniversary of the apology, and will continue to push for tangible actions: for example, moving forward with building the California Indian Heritage Center (CIHC), as promised over twenty years ago.

———

REPRESENTATION AND RE-NAMING

The word Sacramento, which means "most holy sacrament," is loaded with a deep connection to Catholicism and the missionization and colonization of California, always represented as positive within our education system. Re-naming places is an important aspect of a colonizing project; therefore we see this throughout the state and nation. Natives continue to fight for accurate portrayals and new curriculum that includes Natives histories. This is important because an idealized, romanticized, white-washed history is often held as fact. Hence, many of us protesting in Sacramento continue to be met with backlash and ill-informed beliefs about these settlers when their statues are removed.

The momentum from the BLM project has forced us to revisit meaningful conversations surrounding the changing of harmful place names. These harmful place names are not unique to the Sacramento region, but appear across the US. Not only do we see Sutter's name littered across the city, we also bear witness to derogatory place names like [S-word] Valley, which is in the traditional homelands of the Washoe Tribe. (We have chosen not to name these slurs in this article.) While we continue to fight racial slurs in place names, we also continue to fight for the removal of Native people as mascots. Misrepresentation is unfortunately a dominant narrative across the state. In 2015, the California Indian Culture and Sovereignty Center "analyzed 7,169 California Public K–8 schools and identified 78 mascots for a statewide total of 146 public schools with American Indian mascots." As the BLM movement has propelled the renaming of the Washington NFL team, we hope to see continued activism and push for the change of dehumanization of Native peoples as mascots.

———

DE-SUTTER: JUNE 15, 2020

As Sutter is well glorified throughout the Sacramento Valley area, it was important that we first address the historical and contemporary references and continued celebration of Sutter through schools, street names, hospitals, and hotels. The de-Sutter community conversation event was planned for June 16. One day before the community event, we received notice that the statue near the entrance of the Sutter hospital was being removed; hospital officials cited the removal as a "public safety issue."

> To our people, John Sutter is a name that prompts anger and sadness in many, as he was the architect of such destruction against our people. . . . His name will always be a painful part of our people's memory but this removal

and those to follow will provide our people with the much-needed acknowledgement of the State's and Nation's past indiscretions that continue to affect our people today.
—Jesus Tarango, Chairman, Wilton Rancheria

On June 16, Morning Star Gali (Pit River) organized an event to celebrate the removal of Sutter's statue, inviting the Native community to participate and speak about the injustices we have faced for generations. The opening of the celebration began with traditional songs and an opening prayer by tribal elder Albert Titman Sr. (Miwok/Pit River). This significant event allowed a safe space to speak our truths and take a collective step forward in community healing.

> They put us on reservations and rancherias in hopes that we would die. . . . In hopes that we would no longer exist. They stripped us of our language, they tried to take our language. They tried to take our prayer. They tried to take our smudge. They tried to take all these things along with our rights to be human beings . . . and here we are again today. Standing with our Black brothers. With our Brown brothers. They try to divide us by color. They say "you're Black, you're Brown." But we know the truth about who we are. We know who we are. —Albert Titman Sr., Black and Brown Shut It Down event, June 7, 2020

———

DE-SERRA: JULY 4, 2020

After the APTP's peaceful 4th of You Lie: De-Columbus Sacramento protest on July 4, 2020, the crowd's unrest continued to grow. We want to acknowledge that the majority of the protests in Sacramento have been peaceful and filled with a beautiful sense of community, but we also have the right to be angry. The media's portrayal of angry protestors is a false narrative. Don't get us wrong, we are mad—but we want and need change.

> My positionality as a Native American womxn, community member, and a mother to Native children drives my desire to create change and to expose the colonial dynamics of silencing Indigenous presence to further settler claims to land and Indigenous dispossession.
> —Maya Esquivido (Wintu/Hupa)

Junípero Serra is again revered as this "savior" of Indigenous peoples who brought missionization to California, and was even canonized by the Roman Catholic Church in 2015. And again, California Indians work hard to dispel these myths and re-write and re-right this history of forced colonization (Kuruvilla 2015). The first removals of Serra statues were in Golden Gate Park in San Francisco and Father Serra Park in Los Angeles, both toppled on June 19, 2020—Juneteenth. On the Fourth of July, a de-Serra statue removal happened outside of the California state capitol. We heard this was a community removal and want to be careful as there are ongoing investigations. This is a good time to remind people that we need to be cautious of what we say and post on social media— police use these platforms to target our community members for arrest. We continue to see the removal of Junípero Serra statues across the state; on July 23, Ventura County removed their statue of Serra.

> [These are] monuments to racism. These are monuments to genocide. And it's time for them to come down.
> —Morning Star Gali to KQED, July 7, 2020

———

DE-COLUMBUS: JULY 7, 2020

On the morning of July 7, 2020, local Sacramento activists began posting on social media, announcing the removal of the Queen Isabella and Christopher Columbus statue. This rang loudly through the Native community, as the fight to remove this statue had been ongoing since the 1970s (California State Capitol Museum, n.d.). Statue removals evoke a public unsettling of white supremacy, one that is a small part of decolonization and often met with settler resistance. The removal of Columbus was no different: Native supporters of removal were met by a group of Christians in opposition, angry about the uprooting of the Serra statue only three days prior. They continued to advocate for Serra and Columbus: that they brought faith and saved the Indigenous people of California. An interesting juxtaposition of faith and Indigenous history stood here, an old conflict almost replaying in front of the propped-up fence, not separating the groups from each other but from the removal of the state. Native protesters began singing the "Woman Warrior Song" in support of the statue removal to drown out the Christian hymns next to us.

> This moment right here, this moment is for us. This is for our ancestors, this is for my daughter. My daughter is six years old and she will know, she will know that these are murderers. —Vanessa Esquivido to CapRadio, July 7, 2020

———

SOLIDARITY NOT APPROPRIATION

As Black, Brown, and Indigenous folx stand in unity alongside the BLM movement, it is vital to recognize our shared history and the significance of standing in solidarity. The BLM movement and project #BlackLivesMatter were created in 2013 by three queer Black womxn— Alicia Garza, Patrisse Cullors, and Opal Tometi—as a response to the murder of Trayvon Martin and the acquittal of his murderer (Black Lives Matter, n.d.). Seeking justice and demanding accountability, the BLM movement has continued to grow and become unavoidably visible. The Black Trans Lives Matter (BTLM) project has also demanded that their voice be heard. Black LGBTQIA+ people are among the most targeted for violent attacks and it is imperative to recognize the work they have done for the BLM movement. In Sacramento, we have witnessed several events that center LGBTQIA+ Black and Indigenous voices. The BLM and BTLM protests are pivotal, calling attention to social inequality, systemic racism, and other vast injustices created and reinforced through white supremacy.

Restoring Justice for Indigenous Peoples (RJIP), #NativeJusticeNow, is an organization dedicated to serving California Indigenous people in the carceral system. Project director Morning Star Gali works closely with the Native communities affected by mass incarceration.

> We, the Indigenous People of this Land, stand in solidarity with Black Lives Matter. . . . We recognize that the War on Black People is rooted in slavery, which enabled the accumulation of wealth and power needed for the genocide of Native Americans, the founding of the United States, and the colonization of countries throughout the world. The suffering and exploitation that plagues all of our communities is rooted in this history of antiblack racism for the development of capitalism.
> —RJIP, "#BLACKLIVESMATTER Solidarity Statement"

Indigenous voices and histories are often written out of the narrative, overlooked, or purposefully silenced. This is a story that Black folx and Afro-Indigenous communities face too. Essentially, this is not a comparison of oppression(s) but a reckoning of the truth. We need to acknowledge the Afro-Indigenous peoples in our community and the challenges they face holding this space of intersectionality. Antiblackness is the product of colonialism and it continues to perpetuate a racial hierarchy and reinforces the power dynamic of white supremacy (Pérez 2020). It is our individual and collective responsibility to address antiblackness within Indigenous communities and within ourselves.

This can start with addressing the harm perpetuated by the term "Native Lives Matter." Although the phrase has good intentions, it is offensive. BLM is not an exclusion, rather a call for inclusion.

> In this moment, we as Indigenous people need to stand in solidarity with our allies in the Black community and our Afro-Indigenous community as they fight for liberation, equality, and equity; as justice for one is justice for all.
> —Maya Esquivido

———

CALL TO ACTION

This is not an exhaustive list, rather a short list of suggested initial actions:

1. Conversations: If any part of this article makes you uncomfortable, we ask you to investigate why. We encourage you to do your own research on these topics, reach out, have these tough conversions with family and friends.

2. Allyship, not appropriation: Recognize appropriation around Native issues but also how we as Native people can appropriate cultures and movements as well. Be cognizant of the harm to Black communities when we use the phrase "Native Lives Matter"; instead, say "Native Justice Now." Supporting BLM does not take away from Indigenous solidarity— it strengthens, not weakens.

3. Participating: There are plenty of wonderful organizations already doing this work. Seek them out, show up to their events when you can, donate money, offer rides, and/or repost their pages. Sign petitions when you can.

4. Letter writing: Write to your local elected officials about your stance on issues. Demand justice for Breonna Taylor. Learn more: www.untilfreedom.com/breonnataylor.

5. Support: Organizations like Justice Teams Network provide many resources for on-the-ground information. Support local calls for statue removal. Learn more: www.justiceteams.org.

6. Know your rights: The activism that you do is highly important; take care of yourself and know your rights when police stop, question, raid, etc., you. Learn more: www.berkeleycopwatch.org/know-your-rights.

EN LA NOCHE—
IN THE EVENING

URSULA PIKE

Two weeks before training ended, I turned twenty-six. Laura asked where I wanted to celebrate, and I chose Tio Lujo's current site. We weren't sure where Tio Lujo's Bar would be from one weekend to the next. It moved to different spots throughout Cochabamba every few weeks. But the Westerners and expats in town always managed to find it. Information about each new location was spread between rooms at the cheap hostels and restaurants recommended by the travel guidebook everyone carried. *Tio*, which means uncle, ran the bar and was from Argentina, Chile, or one of those other South American countries that didn't seem part of the Third World. His black-rimmed glasses were thick and would have looked ironic in the United States, but in a country where few people could afford glasses, there was no irony. The bar had small tables lit by candles, Spanish music playing on tinny speakers, and a menu of food that was familiar but not very tasty. I never found out why the bar moved around, but suspected it was poor management due to too much Bolivian Marching Powder. Bolivia was full of people from around the world who came specifically for the high-quality, cheap cocaine.

Lujo means luxurious, and no matter what building the bar ended up in, the beers were always more expensive than anywhere else in the city. The bar probably had some other official name, but we called it Tio Lujo.

From the cab we took to Tio Lujo's, we could see the streets filling up with people walking to the Festival of Urkupiña. Devotees of the Virgin Mary made the pilgrimage on foot to the mountain where she had appeared. It was still winter in the Southern Hemisphere, and the pilgrims wore layers of jackets and scarves.

The first round of beers arrived at the table. I hoped someone would bring up the film we all watched during training that afternoon. *Blood of the Condor*, or *Yawar Mallku*, was a 1969 Bolivian film about Quechua villagers and an agency called the Progress Corps. Before starting the film, the training director said, "This movie changed the history of the Peace Corps in Bolivia." All twenty-six of us sat in the large meeting room, which smelled of rice and meat because it was also the lunchroom. We were two weeks from our swearing in—the moment when we held up our hands and promised to represent the United States as Peace Corps volunteers.

The black-and-white film opened with a Bolivian couple in a small earthen-walled room. The wife was young, had smooth skin, and wore a serious expression, but the husband was weathered, and slurred his words. They argued about the death of their children, and the husband blamed the wife for not having another baby. Every word they spoke was in Quechua. I had never seen an entire film in an Indigenous language, and I perked up every time I heard a word I recognized—*warmi* (woman) and *wawa* (baby).

Then the volunteers from the US showed up. Their Spanish was laughable and barely understandable. One woman wore Jackie O sunglasses and pedal pushers. We laughed. Nervously. Those ridiculous people were supposed to be us. I looked around the room. A woman nearby squinted at the screen.

"We, of the Progress Corps, have come here through many sacrifices of our own so that you can develop," the head of the group said to a line of silent, staring village residents. He was a barrel-chested man wearing the same button-up flannel shirt in every scene. He puffed on a pipe as he spoke with controlled condescension to the Bolivians. Boxes of donated clothes were offered to the villagers, who reluctantly accepted the gifts. I thought of the US soldiers who gave blankets infected with smallpox to Native people, and wondered if the filmmaker was saying something about poisoned gifts. Some of the people in the room were paying attention, but more than a few had dozed off. *Are they seeing what I am seeing?* Maybe this was my paranoid Native imagination.

The line about the sacrifices the volunteers were making for the betterment of the Bolivians sounded a little too familiar. No one had stated it so plainly, because our "sacrifice" for the sake of the Bolivians was assumed. Peace Corps volunteers were the most noble motherfuckers on the planet, or so we were told. The more that personal comforts were forgone, the further away we were from a city, from electricity, from toilets and running water, the more valuable was our sacrifice. That sentiment was as true thirty years earlier when the film was made as it was that afternoon in the cafeteria.

In the movie, the women in the village were never able to get pregnant again after visiting the clinic run by the Progress Corps. The film ended when the villagers discovered that the volunteers were "sowing death in the bellies" of the women of the community. It was an allusion to the forced sterilization of the Indigenous women. The North Americans were pulled away into the darkness by the villagers, never to be seen again.

"Remember, this was not based on a real incident," the training director said as he switched off the television. He explained that the movie was shown widely throughout Bolivia in 1970, and it wasn't seen as fiction. Peace Corps was asked to leave the country by the

Bolivian government partly because of the reaction to the movie. Twenty years later, the organization returned, thanks to a government that was friendlier to the United States.

"Do they really think Peace Corps did . . . did this to women?! Is that how they see us?" a woman in the front row asked, her brow crinkled in confusion. Forced sterilization seemed beyond her comprehension. The training director assured us that it never happened and that Peace Corps never operated clinics.

While watching the film, I thought about my mother getting her tubes tied the year I was in fourth grade. I didn't know the term *tubal ligation* at the time, but that's what it was. Her baby-making days were over. She wanted me to know she was choosing it. The afternoon my mother went into the hospital, I stood on the playground imagining giant tubes like multicolored hoses snaking out of her, while a white doctor struggled to tie them together. A few months later, she enrolled in community college.

I was surprised that the other volunteers didn't seem to know that forced sterilization was an actual practice. It wasn't just a perfect metaphor for the genocide Indigenous people had experienced but an actual crime committed on Native women up until the 1970s. In North America, one in four Native women were forcibly sterilized. Full-blooded women were targeted first.

Although I knew that the Peace Corps had never sterilized women, I wasn't surprised that Bolivians were suspicious of the organization's actions. In a world where Indigenous people had been taken advantage of by foreigners and every few decades a new generation showed up promising to help, of course they wouldn't trust volunteers from the US. But I didn't say anything. That evening as I changed my clothes to get ready for my birthday celebration, I wondered what the other trainees would have thought if I'd said I understood why the Bolivians believed the film to be true. Would they see me as unsophisticated and backward? I knew no one would bring up the film on this night of celebration with a handful of days between us and the beginning of our service.

———

From the inside of the bar, I saw that the number of people in the street walking to Urkupiña had doubled in the short time I had been sitting drinking my beer. Laura sat in the seat next to me, and someone said, "Happy Birthday." I thought about bringing up the movie, but what kind of party would it be if I talked about something as horrible as forced sterilization? Laura and I huddled in a corner with a bottle of wine. My time in Kantuta had been demoralizing, but she had had a blast during her visit to southern Bolivia. She had already put a deposit on an apartment. I drank my wine and hoped that I didn't look as dejected as I felt. The bar filled up with volunteers in town for trainings who had heard about the party. I knew it wasn't really for me, but I loved that my party was becoming a big event.

"Hello, who is that?" a woman behind me said, and I looked up to see a scruffy guy with a battered leather hat walk in. It was Daniel, the volunteer from Kantuta who had warned me to stay away. With yellow hair, blue eyes, and dimples, he looked every inch the Southern California surfer dude that he was. I assumed he had no idea who I was, and hoped I wouldn't have to speak to him.

"This must be the birthday girl," he said and wrapped me in a hug. He knew who I was and that I was moving to Kantuta. He had heard about me puking out the back of the sugar cane truck, thanks to Nina. I smiled and tried to think of a witty response, but he disappeared back into the crowd. Laura and I laughed as he stepped away and I was handed a shot glass full of Bolivia's finest *singani*.

At some point I had had too many drinks and knew I needed to leave the building. I didn't want to cry on Laura's shoulder and tell her how much I was going to miss her. Saying no was difficult for me, but I knew I had passed my limit, so I sneaked out the door. I did this anytime I was too drunk to pretend that I was having a good time. Sometimes I needed to be alone. I peeked behind me and was both relieved and heartbroken that no one was coming to save me.

Stumbling out into the street, I bumped into a woman who was heading to Urkupiña. It was nearly midnight, but the wide main boulevard was now full of people. Dogs hiding behind fences barked. Many of the people were carrying toy cars, fake money, and tiny houses. Earlier that night, a taxicab driver told us they were replicas of what the people wanted. When festivalgoers arrived at the hill where the image of la Virgen had appeared, a *yatiri* would bless the replicas, and the people would leave them in hopes of having their specific request filled. The mixture of Indigenous ceremony and Christian icons made me think of the prayer said before powwows I'd attended, thanking Jesus, the Creator, and all our ancestors. I wished I had something a *yatiri* could bless. What could I place on the hill that would help me be the opposite of the smug volunteers in the movie? The three months of training that was about to end had improved my Spanish, taught me a little bit of Quechua, and burned into my mind the shape of Bolivia on a map. But I had no clue as to whether I could help Bolivians. No trinket represented the knowledge I thought I lacked or the experience I hoped to have in Kantuta.

COYOTE TOURS: UNVEILING NATIVE LA

CINDI M. ALVITRE

The Coyote and the Water

A coyote, which, like all the rest of his kin, considered himself as the most austere animal on the face of the earth, not even excepting many himself, came one day to the margin of a small river. Looking over the bank, on seeing the water run so slow, he addressed it in a cunning manner, "What say you to a race?" "Agreed to," answered the water, very calmly. The coyote ran at full speed along the bank until he could hardly stand from fatigue, and on looking over the bank, saw the water running smoothly on.

He walked off with his tail between his legs and had something to reflect on for many a day afterwards.
—*Gabrieleno story collected by Hugo Reid, Los Angeles, 1852*

To the cosmopolitan, Los Angeles is a city with no center and no history, or at least nothing one can visually connect to. The landscape is the work of a feeding frenzy of wily—"wile e"—urban planners, with scattered districts and neighborhoods, strewn-about high-rises, and an occasional green space, all resistant to the Athenian law of isonomy, or a unique center that defines a city. As one of the wealthiest cities on the planet, Los Angeles continues to lure the entrepreneurial coyote, always trying to outrun the river.

To the native—excuse me, native-native—the land is an ever-changing entity, sacred and alive, revealing herself to all those who speak her language. The Indigenous people of the Los Angeles Basin have an intimate connection to the land, water, and creations—a silenced knowing of this city. These silenced knowings challenge perceptions of the present-day City of the Angels.

In the midst of the city of Los Angeles, and beyond, our roots are planted deep beneath the concrete of Beverly Hills mansions. Beneath the dreams of the Hollywood starlet lie the bones of our ancestors. In a city that maintains the largest Native American population in the nation, the Gabrieleno/Tongva remain the smallest tribal population amongst the diaspora of Native American tribes relocated to LA. As a "first contact tribe," we took the initial hits of European intrusion and our populations decreased almost to the point of extinction. And yet here we are, a multiplicity of Tongva communities throughout Los Angeles and Orange Counties, descendants of the survivors of an unspoken genocide that started with the arrival of Spanish missionaries in 1769.

The first nations people of the Los Angeles Basin covered a significant expanse of territory, reaching north to Malibu, traveling into the southern sectors of Orange County and east into Riverside County, including the four Southern Channel Islands. If you ask what we call ourselves, you will receive a number of responses that reflect geography and generational preferences, including Gabrieleno, Mission Indians, Shoshoneans, Tongva, Moompetem, and others. As confusing as it sounds, it actually illustrates that there was a confederation of tribal communities, not a single tribe. You identified yourself based on your village, so if you were from the community of Puvu, the sacred center that marks the emergence of human beings, you would be called a Puvu-vit, individually, or Puvu-vitem, collectively. Add your clan identity, your personal name, and your married name, and there you have it. Pretty simple, right?

Language is at the heart and soul of a worldview. With no fluent speakers, remembering a language relies heavily on the support of other tribes that have experienced similar challenges and linguists who documented the language. Efforts to connect and renew the Tongva language are very much alive, with at least two communities fully engaged in the language revitalization process. Will the Tongva community ever reach a level of complete fluency? As one language learner commented, "We may never reach a level of complete fluency, but to be able to pray and do ceremony in our language is most important."

As unrecognized tribes, we are like ancient rivers prior to industrialization: elusive and without center. We exist in coyote space, an active, complex, and sometimes tragic domain. Controversy and curiosity abound on those rare occasions when we emerge as vessels of history and collide with the modern world!

———

Creating a cartography of coyote space is an act of resistance. Coyote space is about making visible what others cannot, or choose not, to see. Arbitrary political boundaries become meaningless. When they speak of the tribes who lived within what is now the region of Los Angeles, anthropologists separate the Gabrieleno/Tongva from the Tataviam in the east, the Chumash of the north, and the Ajachemem of the south. Yet we are all connected by the navigable paths of the water that emerge from the mountain snows, overflow into the arroyos, feed into the Los Angeles River, merge with the San Gabriel River, and travel along the coastal communities and beyond to the Southern Channel Islands. Water is the lifeblood of the people, and we cannot separate the people from each other, or from the nature, for we are all one and the same.

On the surface, a guided tour of a Tongva LA extends beyond the rigid boundaries of the romanticized California missions and sheds light on towns like Tujunga, Cahuenga, Pacoima, Cucamonga, Topanga, Azusa, and other cities whose names end with "ngna" or "na," which indicate one of hundreds of pre-contact communities, each with their own creation narrative. Tujunga, for example, is a small community in the San Fernando Valley, nestled along the San Gabriel Mountains. Translated from Gabrieleno/Tongva, it is the place of tu'xuu, the old woman, where an immense grandmother monolith has guarded the canyons since time immemorial. Some say she represented a mother earth spirit. As a child, my family regularly took weekly drives and long walks along old trails to visit family. Peering into the deep, clear ponds along Tujunga Canyon was never a simple act when you'd been warned of water spirits that could lure you into the bubbling waters, drawing you into a cosmological abyss that was forever. What? I could never come back?

We can only begin to imagine the world of our ancestors. Theirs is a topography that challenges the perceptions of those educated within the Western paradigm. The Tongva see a dimensional space with an upper world, middle world, and under world, all occupied by beings that protect the precarious ecology of their realm. Humans, for example, occupy the middle world and are the last of the ancestral dreamtime, created not to control the hunukvitem, the pre-humans, but to take care of all that existed prior to us.

Even for the most recent generations, gathering acorns for weewish in expansive oak groves, harvesting acorns and berries in lush canyons, hunting deer in the thickets of the local mountains, and collecting medicine plants along the creeks and rivers are all perceived as the obligations of stewards of the land. This stewardship bands us together to protect the sacred urban landscape. Our elders define their very identities by environmental markers, and they become disgruntled and frustrated when villages and trails are replaced with streets and neighborhoods that have no resemblance to their memories of the land. My heart recalls the words of my father when he would see these changes. Heartbroken, he would say, "I want to go home."

———

LOCATING YAANGNA

Ultimately, it is about the land. As the original people of the land, we feel our mother earth. Her health reflects our health . . . if she is suffering, so are we.
—*Craig Torres, descendant of Yaangna*

Where is home? An attempt to map Tongva LA is a futile act unless people are brave enough to listen to a tragic history.

Yaangna was the principal ancestral village that moved along the Los Angeles River for countless generations, before the water was confined and silenced within a concrete sarcophagus, separating the people from that which gives life. In pre-contact times people moved slowly, with the seasons, the food, and, ultimately, the water. Colonization and missionization accelerated the pace of relocation as Native people tried to outrun the colonizers, always clinging to the river. After the secularization of the missions, Native people were cultural prisoners-of-war, released from generations of confinement into a permanently altered existence. Yaangna became a refugee camp for tribal families seeking some sense of tradition. Its inhabitants also took in relatives from the islands, the Pipimares, after they were forcibly relocated from Santa Catalina and other Channel Islands from 1816 to 1820.

The final blow to historic Yaangna took place in 1847, after it had been relocated multiple times from one side of the river to the other. On a cold fall evening in 1847, the last generation of Yavitem were turned out onto Calle de los Negros, the place of the dark ones, after their village was razed to the ground by the Los Angeles City Council. Since 1836, the Regidor of the Committee on Zanjas had received complaints like this one: "[residents] were compelled to drink water from the main zanja [where] Indians wash and bathe." Offended by the Indians' wildness and use of the water in the zanja, citizens of the Pueblo finally succeeded in extinguishing any displays of tradition . . . or sharing of common water.

Secularization of Mission San Gabriel had had dire consequences, and Yaangna had been the last traditional holdout of Indigenous refugees, disenfranchised souls displaced by settler colonialism. The land was no longer the open expanse that had sustained the people. The abundance of steelhead shimmering in the river, the round hillsides dotted with oak trees and cottonwoods, the environment of subsistence—all were replaced by geometric layers of brick and mortar. Indian Mary was left to wander the streets.

The last documented location of Yaangna likely stood on a site that is now marked by nothing more than a center divider on the Hollywood Freeway at the intersection of North Alameda and Aliso Street. Yaangna may be buried beneath a gentrified LA, but somehow its soul continues to travel through the city. Craig Torres and I were leaving the city after a late-night Ancestor ceremony at the FarmLab. Unfamiliar with the city, we found ourselves driving down narrow, dimly lit side streets, where we saw hundreds of homeless people, refugees of economic and social disenfranchisement, darkened silhouettes seeking respite from the chill of winter cold along the greasy pavement. It was a haunting déjà-vu moment: our families experienced this 166 years ago. Time, unresolved intergenerational grief, and the present collided. These memories cling to the soul and are often triggered by the human tragedy and suffering that persists in Los Angeles. Los Angeles has an old soul, one that few will recognize and fewer will experience.

—

FIELDS OF HOPI CORN: FARMLAB

In the history of Native Los Angeles, significant individuals have become iconic in their actions and their suffering. At the top of that list is Toypurina, a young woman and sabia, one with exceptional wisdom, from the village of Japchibit. In 1785, at the tender age of twenty-five, she, along with others (including a neophyte named Nicolas José), reacted to the colonial takeover of their homeland by planning to take over Mission San Gabriel. The revolt was intercepted after one of the guards was forewarned of the plot. Punishment was doled out: the men received lashes and Toypurina, the sole woman, was exiled to Monterey, removed from her homeland forever.

Toypurina has become an icon to many, including young Chicanas, who see her as a champion of historic brown feminism in the City of the Angels. Her imagined portrait has been incorporated into neighborhood murals and stenciled in sacred black, white, and red by clandestine guerrilla artists throughout the city.

Generations later, her few descendants have traveled south, seeking to reconnect to their ancestral homeland. Linda, a descendant granddaughter of Toypurina, journeyed from San Juan Bautista to meet members of the Tongva community and participate in a ceremony on the land at the FarmLab, acknowledged by many Tongva as a center of revitalization and the closest connection to the original Yaangna and the Los Angeles River.

Located just north of Chinatown, the FarmLab, or Anabolic Monument, is a ceremonial center and cultural phenomenon in the northern sector of the city. Now part of the Los Angeles State Historic Park, the thirty-two-acre site ("The Cornfield" in the local vernacular) was an industrial brownfield until artist Lauren Bon, along with generous community members, removed decades of industrial waste and toxic soils, replaced them with cleansed earth, and saturated the landscape with feathery tassels of hand-planted Hopi corn.

Those who had the honor of meeting Linda hung on her every word as she shared details and thoughts about her grandmother's traumatic experience and expulsion from her homeland by the Spanish courts. Linda's words were a recognition of shared experiences of the land.

If you sit on the land long enough, and quietly enough, you will hear her speak. And if you build a ceremonial lodge in the midst of downtown, in the middle of a cornfield . . . you will hear the water speak, a once fluid voice now permanently confined in a cement vault. Her voice moves through the hearts of the lodgepoles and the willows gathered along a clandestine creek in Eagle Rock. The sacred volcanic rocks crackle as the heat rises against the heavy canvas tarp, seeping into the lodgepoles, reviving the life of the wood, rehydrating an ancient memory absorbed from the river, where the water of Yaangna is confined. She wants to be free, she speaks to those who will listen.

———

HARAMOKNGNA: RETRACING AN ANCIENT PATH OUT OF THE INDUSTRIAL WILDERNESS

Ancient foot trails became roads, which became freeways, erasing the original footsteps of the ancestors as they traveled to gather, harvest, exchange, and visit with their relatives in the mountains. I envy the health of the ancestors, especially the runners, as they made their way up the mountainous trails sustained only by water and chia seed. I can see their deerskin pouches bouncing along, dropping seeds that will perhaps successfully propagate, marking the trail and providing sustenance to the people.

Runners travel in both directions, to the mountains and to the ocean. At the head of the Arroyo Seco is the site of Hahamongna. A winding trail welcomes the visitor, now earth citizen, to refocus and embrace the natural legacy of the land. Travel further and deeper into the mountain forest along the San Gabriel Trail, or the Angeles Crest Highway, and you will come upon Haramokngna, a living cultural center nestled atop Mount Wilson. It is a point of intersection for the five tribes of the San Gabriel Mountains—the Tongva, Tataviam, Serrano, Kitanemuk, and Chumash—where tribal communities come together to harvest pine nuts, teas, or medicine plants that grow at higher elevations. Deep, wintery snowdrifts and raging forest fires are reminders of the delicate balance of life and destruction. We are reminded to both give life and take life.

At Haramokngna, traditions have been revived, demonstrating the resilience of the people. If you visit on a day when they are cooking, your Angeleno palate will be transformed. Thanks to the ethnobotanical wisdom of Native educators such as Barbara Drake, Abe Sanchez, and Craig Torres, a Chia Café of sorts is at your service. The native food is a joyous choreography of yucca blossoms, chia seed, deer stew, and mesquite tortillas, and it proudly announces a return to healthful ways of living and the shedding of colonial byproducts that have contributed to First World diseases, such as the diabetes, hypertension, and heart disease that have devastated Native American people. Yucca blossoms, anyone?

———

MOOMAT AHIKO: BREATH OF THE OCEAN

One day the fish were discussing ways to create more room for themselves as their number had become so great. Along came a large fish carrying the rock Toshaawt, which he broke open. In the center was a ball filled with gall, which emptied into the water. Soon the stream became salty and bitter and it overflowed the earth to become the present oceans.
—*Geronimo Boscana, Chinichich (1933, 31–32)*

Historically, the Los Angeles River converged with the San Gabriel and continued on to the sacred center of the Tongva world, Puvungna, and on to the Southern Channel Islands, said to the be land of the oldest and most powerful of all Southern California tribes. Coastal zones continue to be active cultural regions where Tongva communities have renegotiated urban space to create living cultural centers such as at Puvungna, a ceremonial center now located at California State University, Long Beach. And every once in a while, ancestors reveal themselves in dreams.

Moomat Ahiko is my story. On one of those hot summer nights when sleep is a rare commodity, my deepest longing for the ocean called an island warrior into my dreamtime. The shimmer of abalone beads caught my glance. His enormous brown shoulders were embedded in granite and soil, each a peak of the Santa Ana Mountains. His wet, black hair was pulled up on his deep burrowed forehead and his eyes were closed in meditation. Lava spewed out of his third eye, the sacred space between the eyebrows. My children were playfully tossing chunks of lava to each other. I watched in disbelief, well aware as a single mother of four that exhaustion plays tricks on the mind, even in dreamtime. Now there was a vast body of water filled with wooden planked canoes, and in each of the canoes were family and community members. We began to sing, counting each stroke as we paddled towards the warrior. And when we were all in unison, the warrior opened his eyes, the lava stopped, and the mountains opened like a magnificent door to reveal Catalina Island. We pulled the water, stroke by stroke, towards the island. I woke up, stunned and in disbelief, wondering what it all meant. Was it a dream or a vision?

I awakened not knowing how something so magnificent could be real. Weeks later, a gentleman who was knowledgeable about Southern California Indian maritime culture called with a generous offer to build a ti'at. *Moomat Ahiko, Breath of the Ocean,* was born, the first traditional Tongva plank canoe in over 150 years. She has become an icon and an inspiration to the Coastal and Island tribal communities; maritime tradition was considered to be extinct. As I write this, the Chumash are preparing to launch their tomols and journey to Limuw (Santa Cruz Island), their ancestral homeland off the Santa Barbara coast. It is a joyous time to inspire and be inspired. The revival of maritime culture has also renewed relationships with Pacific Island communities that share this vast expanse of sacredness.

———

The legacy of Yaangna and the silenced Los Angeles River have played out for well over two hundred years, through successive onslaughts of Spaniards, Catholic missionaries, Mexican rancheros, and Yankees. Seemingly all roads lead to Yaangna, like rivers to the ocean. Yaangna continues as a refugee space in the northern sectors of the city where immigrants, cosmopolitans, and guests seek acceptance and a place to call "home." As a historic site, she remains multiplicious and undefined. Yet there are those who come to know her inclusiveness in revived sectors such as the FarmLab. Her descendants work to restore her reputation, to make her visible and free of rusting colonial memory. This happens in increments, just as the native plant garden at the Anabolic Monument, perpetually in a state of transformation, becomes medicine for all. The FarmLab and Haramokngna have become ceremonial centers of contemporary Los Angeles, providing sustenance to refugees from many tribes. It is all we have as a landless people, but we share.

Coyote has found his way into the city once again, doing his magic and admitting to his own foolishness. How do the Tongva navigate through life? Look up at grandmother moon, look down at mother earth, and always thank the water.

REFERENCES
AND NOTES

Some of the essays include bibliographic references or other notes. Where applicable, those notes are included here.

Michael Connolly Miskwish, "Hutnyilshs: The Black Dog Nation"

Barajas, Dení Trejo, and Marie Christine Duggan. 2018. "San Blas and the Californias: Hispanic Trade in the Northern Pacific Rim in a Time of Great Change (1767–1820)." *Mains'l Haul* 54: 28–47.

Beebe, Rose Marie, and Robert Senkewicz, trans. and ed. 2013. "On the Road to San Diego: Junípero Serra's Baja California Diary." *Journal of San Diego History* 59, no. 4 (Fall): 189–240.

Carrico, Richard L. 1990. "Spanish Crime and Punishment: The Native American Experience in Colonial San Diego, 1760–1830." *Western Legal History* 3 (1): 21–33.

Duggan, Marie Christine. 2016. "With and Without an Empire: Financing for California Missions Before and After 1810." *Pacific Historical Review* 85, no. 1 (February): 23–71.

Killea, Lucy Lytle. 1966. "The Political History of a Mexican Pueblo: San Diego from 1825 to 1845—Part II." *Journal of San Diego History* 12 (3): 17–40.

Kino, Eusebio Francisco. 1919. *Kino's Historical Memoir of Pimería Alta: A Contemporary Account of the Beginnings of California, Sonora, and Arizona, 1683–1711.* Translated and edited by Herbert Eugene Bolton. Cleveland: Arthur H. Clark Company.

Lacson, P. Albert. 2015. "Making Friends and Converts: Cloth and Clothing in Early California History." *California History* 92 (1): 6–26.

McDonald, William E. 1934. "The Pious Fund of the Californias." *The Catholic Historical Review* 19, no. 4 (January): 427–436.

Meigs, Peveril I. 1935. *The Dominican Mission Frontier of Lower California.* Berkeley: University of California Press.

Panich, Lee M. 2010. "Spanish Missions in the Indigenous Landscape: A View from Mission Santa Catalina, Baja California." *Journal of California and Great Basin Anthropology* 30 (1): 69–86.

Panich, Lee M. 2017. "Indigenous Vaqueros in Colonial California: Labor, Identity, and Autonomy." In *Foreign Objects: Rethinking Indigenous Consumption in American Archaeology,* edited by Craig N. Cipolla, 187–203. Tucson: University of Arizona Press.

Powell, Philip Wayne. 1952. *Soldiers, Indians, and Silver: The Northward Advance of New Spain,* 1550–1600. Berkeley: University of California Press.

Rojo, Manuel C. (1879) 1972. *Historical Notes on Lower California with Some Relative to Upper California Furnished to the Bancroft Library by Manuel C. Rojo.* Edited by Philip O. Gericke. Los Angeles: Dawson's Book Shop, 1972.

Santa Maria, Guillermo de. 2003. *Guerra de los chichimecas: (México 1575—Zirosto 1580).* Zamora, Guadalajara, Los Lagos: Universidad de Guadalajara, Universitario Los Lagos, El Colegio de San Luis.

Schmal, John P. 2003. "The Indigenous People of Zacatecas: The Ancestors of Today's Mexican Americans." *LatinoLA,* July 17, 2003. latinola.com/story.php?story=1109.

Rose Soza War Soldier, "Speaking Out: Rupert Costo and the American Indian Historical Society"

American Indian Historical Society. 1964a. Preliminary Organization Meeting for the Founding of American Indian Historical Society, July 14, 1964. Costo papers, Collection 170, Box 12, folder 9. University of California, Riverside.

American Indian Historical Society. 1964b. Minutes of American Indian Historical Society meeting, August 21, 1964. Costo papers, Collection 170, Box 12, folder 9. University of California, Riverside.

American Indian Historical Society. 1965. Executive Council Meeting Minutes, December 10, 1965. Costo papers, Collection 170, Box 12, folder 10. University of California, Riverside.

American Indian Historical Society. 1969. Executive Council Meeting Minutes, January 3, 1969. Costo papers, Collection 170, Box 12, folder 14. University of California, Riverside.

"The Chautauqua Spokesman." 1967. *The Indian Historian* 4 (January/February).

Costo, Rupert. 1966. "The Right to Leadership." *The Indian Historian* 3 (March): 14.

Costo, Rupert. 1967. "Fact from Fiction." *The Indian Historian* 4 (January/February).

Costo, Rupert. 1970. "Alcatraz." *The Indian Historian* 3 (Winter).

Costo, Rupert. 1977. "Speaking Freely: Tribal Sovereignty." *Wassaja*, February 1977.

Costo, Rupert, and Jeannette Henry-Costo. 1995. *Natives of the Golden State: The California Indians*. San Francisco: The Indian Historian Press and the University of California at Riverside.

Drew, William J. 1926. "Educational Provisions for California Indians." *Transactions of the Commonwealth Club of California* 21 (June 8, 1926): 115.

"Education Study Begins." 1965. *The Indian Historian* 2 (June/July): 10.

Hillinger, Charles. 1977. "Indian Couple Spread the Native American Word." *The Los Angeles Times*, November 14, 1977, A3.

"Indian Society." 1967. *San Francisco Chronicle*, June 21, 1967, 48.

"Indians among the Hippies." 1967. *San Francisco Chronicle*, March 3, 1967.

Ohlone Indians of California. 1970. Petition to President Richard Nixon, January 22, 1970. White House Central Files, Subject File IN (Jan 1–March 31, 1970), Box 5, File 1 of 2.

"Workshop on Indian at Berkeley." 1966. *Oakland Tribune*, November 8, 1966, 18.

Cutcha Risling Baldy, "The G-O Road: Thirty Years Later"

This article could not have been completed without the research and help of Jenifer Hailey (Hoopa Valley Tribe), a student and Native American studies major at Humboldt State University. Quotes from this article were taken from a podcast created by Humboldt State University students Marlene' Dusek (Payómkawichum/Ipai), Charley Reed (Karuk/Hupa/Yurok), and Gabriel Goff for NAS 325: Tribes of California. Additional quotes were taken from an interview with Chris Peters, "The No-GO Road 30 Years Later," which aired on KHSU on April 26, 2018.

Cutcha Risling Baldy, "Water Is Life: The Flower Dance Ceremony"

Parts of this interview are also included in the author's book *We Are Dancing for You: Native Feminisms and the Revitalization of Women's Coming-of-Age Ceremonies*, published by University of Washington Press in 2018.

Save California Salmon, "California Can't Promise Truth and Healing While Forcing the Salmon into Extinction"

Two Rivers Tribune staff contributed to this essay. For more information, please visit www.californiasalmon.org or follow Save California Salmon on Facebook, Instagram, and Twitter.

Michelle L. LaPena and Viola LeBeau, "The West Berkeley Shellmound: A Legal Battle That Has Inspired a Generation"

Dinkelspiel, Frances. 2016. "Second West Berkeley Human Remains Discovery Prompts Call to Re-examine Shellmound Boundaries." *Berkeleyside*, May 11, 2016. www.berkeleyside. org/2016/05/11/second-west-berkeley-human-remains-discovery-prompts-call-to-re-examine-shellmound-boundaries.

Hicks, Tony. 2019. "Berkeley Approves Two Affordable Housing Projects in Record Time under New State Law, SB35." *Berkeleyside*, January 17, 2019. www.berkeleyside.org/2019/01/17/berkeley-approves-two-affordable-housing-projects-in-record-time-under-new-state-law-sb-35.

Johnson, Hal. 1942. "So, We're Told." *Berkeley Daily Gazette*, December 30, 1942.

National Trust for Historic Preservation. 2020. "Discover America's 11 Most Endangered Historic Places for 2020." September 24, 2020. www.savingplaces.org/stories/discover-americas-11-most-endangered-historic-places-for-2020.

Ruegg & Ellsworth et al. v. City of Berkeley et al. Alameda County Superior Court No. RG18930003. April 20, 2021.

Shellmound. 2019. "Court Victory: Judge Rules against Shellmound Developers." October 24, 2019. shellmound.org/2019/10/court-victory.

Shellmound. 2020. "Berkeley Shellmound Site Listed as One of America's 11 Most Endangered Historic Places." September 24, 2020. shellmound.org/2020/09/11most.

Shellmound. 2021. "State Appeals Court Hears Arguments to Erase West Berkeley Shellmound." February 17, 2021. shellmound.org/2021/02/state-appeals-court-press-release.

Shellmound. n.d. "Learn More." Accessed May 30, 2021. shellmound.org/learn-more.

Wollenberg, Charles. 2008. *Berkeley: A City in History*. Berkeley: University of California Press.

Rose Soza War Soldier, "Teaching about Race in a University"

Burnett, Peter H. 1851. "Governor's Annual Message to the Legislature, January 7, 1851." Accessed July 16, 2018. governors.library.ca.gov/addresses/s_01-Burnett2.html.

Gabe's 4th Grade "Mission" Project. 2015. FNX First Nations Experience. vimeo.com/136237208.

"The Indian Side of a War Question." 1861. *Marysville Daily Appeal*, December 7, 1861, 2.

"Indian Slavery." 1862. *Daily Alta California*, April 14, 1862, 1.

Rose Soza War Soldier, "California Indians and California Love: Belonging, Kinship, and Land"

Bancroft, Hubert Howe. 1886. *Wild Tribes*. Vol. 1 of *The Native Races*. San Francisco: The History Company Publishers.

Bauer, William J., Jr. 2016. *California through Native Eyes: Reclaiming History*. Seattle: University of Washington Press.

Costo, Rupert. 1977. "Fact from Fiction." *The Indian Historian* 10, no. 1 (Winter): 31–36.

Garroutte, Eva Marie. 2003. *Real Indians: Identity and the Survival of Native America*. Berkeley: University of California Press.

Helper, Hinton Rowan. 1855. *The Land of Gold: Reality versus Fiction*. Baltimore: H. Taylor.

Holm, Tom, J. Diane Pearson, and Ben Chavis. 2003. "Peoplehood: A Model for the Extension of Sovereignty in American Indian Studies." *Wicazo Sa Review* 18, no. 1: 7–24.

Lang, Julian. 2002. "The Cid." In *Urban Voices: The Bay Area American Indian Community*, ed. Susan Lobo, 149–152. Tucson: University of Arizona Press.

Miranda, Deborah A. 2013. *Bad Indians: A Tribal Memoir*. Berkeley: Heyday.

Payson, George. 1853. *Golden Dreams and Leaden Realities*. New York: G. P. Putnam & Co.

Smith, Linda Tuhiwai. 1999. *Decolonizing Methodologies: Research and Indigenous Peoples*. London: Zed Books.

TallBear, Kim. 2013. *Native American DNA: Tribal Belonging and the False Promise of Genetic Science*. Minneapolis: University of Minnesota Press.

Vanessa Esquivido, Maya Esquivido, and Morning Star Gali, "Black Lives Matter on Indigenous Land: Solidarity in Sacramento"

Black Lives Matter. n.d. "Herstory." Accessed August 22, 2020. blacklivesmatter. com/herstory.

California Indian Heritage Center Foundation. n.d. Accessed August 22, 2020. www.cihcfoundation.org.

California State Capitol Museum. n.d. "Queen Isabella: A Gift of Generosity and Controversy." Accessed August 22, 2020. www.capitolmuseum. ca.gov/ exhibits-and-collections/queen-isabella.

Kuruvilla, Carol. 2020. "Native Americans in California Are Toppling Statues of this Catholic Saint." *HuffPost*, June 26, 2020, updated June 29, 2020. www.huffpost.com/entry/junipero-serra-statue-protests-catholic_n_ 5ef4 b611c5b66c3126832dff.

Lindsay, Brendan. 2012. *Murder State: California's Native American Genocide, 1846–1873.* Lincoln: University of Nebraska Press.

Nixon, Andrew, and Kris Vera-Phillips. 2020. "Christopher Columbus Statue Removed from California State Capitol Rotunda." CapRadio, July 7, 2020. www.capradio.org/articles/2020/07/07/christopher-columbus-statue-removed-from-california-state-capitol-rotunda.

Pérez, Ana Cecilia. 2020. "As Non-Black POC, We Need to Address Anti-Blackness." *Yes!*, July 6, 2020. www.yesmagazine.org/opinion/ 2020/07/06/non-black-poc-anti-blackness.

Proudfit, Joely. 2015. "Cultural Appropriation in California Public K–12 Schools: Tribal Mascots and Stereotypes." California Indian Culture and Sovereignty Center, California State University San Marcos. www.csusm.edu/ cicsc/projects/gis-projects.html.

Restoring Justice for Indigenous Peoples. n.d. "#BLACKLIVESMATTER Solidarity Statement." Accessed August 22, 2020. www.indigenousjustice.org/ solidarity.

Severn, Carly. 2020. "'How Do We Heal?' Toppling the Myth of Junípero Serra." KQED, July 7, 2020. www.kqed.org/news/11826151/how-do-we-heal-toppling-the-myth-of-junipero-serra.

Tuck, Eve, and K. Wayne Yang. 2012. "Decolonization Is Not a Metaphor." *Decolonization: Indigeneity, Education, and Society* 1, no. 1: 1–40.

PERMISSIONS

"Saging the World" copyright © 2020, 2022 by Rose Ramirez and Deborah Small, originally published in *News from Native California*, Spring 2020, and expanded for this book. Reprinted by permission of Rose Ramirez and Deborah Small.

"The G-O Road: Thirty Years Later" copyright © 2018 by Cutcha Risling Baldy, originally published in *News from Native California*, Fall 2018. "Water Is Life: The Flower Dance Ceremony" copyright © 2017 by Cutcha Risling Baldy, originally published in *News from Native California*, Spring 2017. Reprinted by permission of Cutcha Risling Baldy.

"Water and Oil" copyright © 2017 by Michelle L. LaPena, originally published in *News from Native California*, Spring 2017. Reprinted by permission of Michelle L. LaPena.

"California Can't Promise Truth and Healing While Forcing the Salmon into Extinction" copyright © 2021 by Save California Salmon, originally published in *News from Native California*, Fall 2021. Reprinted by permission of Save California Salmon.

"The West Berkeley Shellmound: A Legal Battle That Has Inspired a Generation" copyright © 2021 by Michelle L. LaPena and Viola LeBeau, originally published in *News from Native California*, Summer 2021. Reprinted by permission of Michelle L. LaPena and Viola LeBeau.

"Education as Self-Determination" © 2013, 2022 by Olivia Chilcote and Chris Medellin, originally published in *News from Native California*, Winter 2013/14. Revised and expanded version reprinted by permission of Olivia Chilcote and Chris Medellin.

"Creating Ceremonies to Protect Us from Traumatic Research" copyright © 2019 by Maura Sullivan. Originally published in *News from Native California*, Summer 2019. Reprinted by permission of Maura Sullivan.

"A Word with Chiitaanibah Johnson" copyright © 2016 by Vincent Medina, originally published in *News from Native California*, Winter 2015/16.

"My University, My Ancestors" copyright © 2022 by Emily Clarke. Reprinted by permission of Emily Clarke.

ABOUT THE CONTRIBUTORS

Terria Smith is the editor of *News from Native California* magazine and director of the Berkeley Roundhouse, Heyday's California Indian publishing program. She is a tribal member of the Torres Martinez Desert Cahuilla Indians in Southern California and an alum of the UC Berkeley Graduate School of Journalism.

Deborah A. Miranda is an enrolled member of the Ohlone/Costanoan-Esselen Nation of the Greater Monterey Bay Area in California, with Santa Ynez Chumash ancestry. She is the author of *Bad Indians: A Tribal Memoir*, published by Heyday in 2013. She is also the author of four poetry collections and coeditor of *Sovereign Erotics: A Collection of Two-Spirit Literature*. She earned her Ph.D. in English literature from the University of Washington in Seattle and was professor of English at Washington and Lee University, where she taught literature of the margins and creative writing. She retired from her professorship in 2021 to focus on scholarship and poetry involving California mission history and literatures. She and her spouse, writer Margo Solod, live in Eugene, Oregon, a short distance from her homelands in California.

Greg Sarris is currently serving his fifteenth term as chairman of the Federated Indians of Graton Rancheria. His publications include *Keeping Slug Woman Alive* (1993), *Mabel McKay: Weaving the Dream* (1994, reissued 2013), *Grand Avenue* (1994, reissued 2015), *Watermelon Nights* (1998, reissued 2021), *How a Mountain Was Made* (2017, published by Heyday), and *Becoming Story* (2022, published by Heyday). Greg lives and works in Sonoma County, California. Visit his website at greg-sarris.com.

Michael Connolly Miskwish (Campo Band of Kumeyaay) served for seventeen years in elected office for the Campo Kumeyaay Nation and helped establish and directed one of the first tribal environmental protection agencies in the United States. Michael has researched and implemented traditional environmental practices in contemporary land and resource management and worked on environmental policy for the National Congress of American Indians, National Tribal Environmental Council, and several EPA advisory committees. He is adjunct faculty of American

Indian studies at San Diego State University, and his work on issues of taxation policy and impediments to sustainable tribal economies is nationally recognized. He has published two books on Kumeyaay history and one on Kumeyaay cosmology.

Deborah Dozier is the author of *The Heart Is Fire: The World of the Cahuilla Indians of Southern California*, published by Heyday in 1998.

Rose Soza War Soldier (Mountain Maidu/Cahuilla/Luiseño) is an enrolled member of the Soboba Band of Luiseño Indians. She completed a B.A. in history with a double minor in political science and social/ethnic relations at UC Davis and a Ph.D. in history with an emphasis in American Indian history from Arizona State University. She is a faculty member in the ethnic studies department at California State University, Sacramento. Her research and teaching focus on twentieth-century American Indian activism, social and cultural history, politics, education, and justice-centered movements.

Jayden Lim is an award-winning Pomo activist and leader who currently serves as a tribal youth ambassador for the California Indian Museum and Cultural Center, located in Santa Rosa. She is currently an undergraduate student at Stanford University and is pursuing two majors: comparative studies in race and ethnicity with a focus on politics, policy, and equity; and history, with a focus on American law. Apart from this, she is skilled in GIS software, business planning, Pomo language documentation, and graphic design, and she is a DJ on the side. She is passionate about food sovereignty, Missing and Murdered Indigenous Women, education, and criminal justice.

River Garza is an artist from Los Angeles, California, whose work draws on traditional Indigenous aesthetics, Southern California Indigenous maritime culture, skateboarding, graffiti, Mexican culture, and lowrider culture.

Rose Ramirez (Chumash/Yaqui descent) is an artist, basketweaver, photographer, and educator. She is a coauthor of *Ethnobotany Project: Contemporary Uses of Native Plants of Southern California and Northern Baja California Indians* (bilingual English/Spanish edition, Malki Museum Press, 2018). She is also one of the producers and directors of the 2022 documentary *Saging the World*.

Deborah Small is an artist, photographer, and professor emerita at California State University, San Marcos. With Rose Ramirez she is a coauthor of *Ethnobotany Project* as well as a coproducer and codirector of *Saging the World*.

Cutcha Risling Baldy is an assistant professor of Native American studies at Cal Poly Humboldt. Her research is focused on Indigenous feminisms, California Indians, environmental justice, and decolonization. Her book *We Are Dancing for You: Native Feminisms and the Revitalization of Women's Coming-of-Age Ceremonies*, published by University of Washington Press in 2018, was awarded Best First Book in Native American and Indigenous Studies at the 2019 Native American and Indigenous Studies Association conference. She received her Ph.D. in Native American studies with a designated emphasis in feminist theory and research from the University of California, Davis, and her M.F.A. in creative writing and literary research from San Diego State University. She also has a B.A. in psychology from Stanford University. She is Hupa, Yurok, and Karuk, and is an enrolled member of the Hoopa Valley Tribe in Northern California.

Michelle L. LaPena (Pit River Tribe) is a mother of three and Indian law attorney. She has lectured at primary, secondary, and university levels and published a number of essays and nonfiction and law review articles on topics related to California Indians and federal Indian law. She received her B.A. in 1993 and her J.D. in 1998, both from the University of California, Davis. In 2017 she received her M.F.A. in creative writing at the Institute of American Indian Arts and she is a recipient of the 2015 Truman Capote Creative Writing Fellowship and the American Indian College Fund's Full Circle Scholarship.

Save California Salmon is dedicated to protecting and restoring the Salmon, Klamath, Trinity, Sacramento, Eel, and Smith Rivers, through restoring flows and salmon habitat, removing dams, and improving water quality; fighting new threats to rivers such as new dams, diversions, and pipelines; and empowering people to fight for rivers and salmon.

Viola LeBeau (Hammawi Band of the Pit River Nation; Cahuilla/Maidu/Cheyenne River Sioux descendent) is a visual multimedia artist and advocate of traditional knowledge. She received her B.A. in sociology and studio arts from Mills College and now works on community outreach, directorial assistance, and food distribution issues with Sogorea Te' Land Trust.

Olivia Chilcote is a member of the San Luis Rey Band of Mission Indians and an assistant professor of American Indian studies at San Diego State University. She earned her Ph.D. and M.A. in ethnic studies at UC Berkeley and her B.A. in ethnic and women's studies at Cal Poly Pomona. Her research and teaching focus on the areas of interdisciplinary Native American studies, California Indian history, federal Indian law and policy, and Native American identity. She grew up in the center of her tribe's traditional territory in the North County of San Diego and she is active in tribal politics and other community efforts. She was a first-generation college student and the first person in her tribe to earn a Ph.D.

Chris Medellin and his family are from the Tule River tribe of Yokuts of central California. Raised in San Diego, as a first-generation college student he earned a bachelor's degree in television, film, and new media and American Indian studies and a master's degree in postsecondary educational leadership with a specialization in student affairs, both from San Diego State University (SDSU). He is currently pursuing a Ph.D. in education at SDSU and Claremont Graduate University. After working his way through various roles on campus, including student assistant, administrative support, and outreach coordinator, he currently serves as the inaugural director of the SDSU Native Resource Center. He is also president of the American Indian Alumni Chapter of San Diego State and founding member of SDSU's Native American and Indigenous Faculty Staff Association and the Men of Color Alliance.

Maura Sullivan (Coastal Band of the Chumash Nation, Slek'en hi šišilop) is from Ventura. She is currently a Ph.D. student in the linguistics program at Tulane University in New Orleans and earned a bachelor's degree in art history and Native American studies from UC Berkeley in 2012.

Vincent Medina (East Bay Ohlone) is a cofounder, with Louis Trevino, of the community organization mak-'amham/Cafe Ohlone. From 2013 to 2016 he was the Roundhouse outreach coordinator for Heyday and *News from Native California*.

Emily Clarke is a Cahuilla writer, bead artist, activist, cordage instructor, and traditional bird dancer. In her free time Emily runs her small business, Cahuilla Woman Creations, performs her work at various events, and coedits her literary journal, *Rejected Lit*. She is the 2022–23 Graton Roundhouse intern for Heyday and *News from Native California*.

Vanessa Esquivido (Nor Rel Muk Wintu/Hupa) is an assistant professor of American Indian studies at CSU Chico.

Maya Esquivido (Nor Rel Muk Wintu/Hupa) is a teaching and curriculum design fellow at Seattle Central College. She has a master's of social work, with a graduate certificate in American Indian and Indigenous studies, from the University of Washington.

Morning Star Gali (Ajumawi Band of Pit River) is the project director at Restoring Justice for Indigenous Peoples (www.indigenousjustice.org).

Ursula Pike is a graduate of the M.F.A. program at the Institute of American Indian Arts and the author of *An Indian among los Indígenas: A Native Travel Memoir* (Heyday, 2021). Her work won the 2019 Writers' League of Texas Manuscript Contest in the memoir category and her writing has appeared in *Literary Hub*, *Yellow Medicine Review*, *World Literature Today*, and *Ligeia Magazine*. She has an M.A. in economics, with a focus on community economic development, and was a Peace Corps volunteer in Bolivia from 1994 to 1996. An enrolled member of the Karuk Tribe, she was born in California and grew up in Daly City, California, and Portland, Oregon. She currently lives in Austin, Texas.

Cindi M. Alvitre is a mother and grandmother and has been an educator and artist-activist for over three decades. She is a descendant of the original inhabitants of Los Angeles and Orange Counties. In 1985 she and Lorene Sisquoc cofounded Mother Earth Clan, a collective of Indian women who created a model for cultural and environmental education. In the late 1980s she cofounded the Ti'at Society, sharing in the renewal of ancient maritime practices of the coastal and island Tongva. She is the author of the children's book *Waa'aka': The Bird Who Fell in Love with the Sun* (Heyday, 2020). She currently teaches American Indian studies at California State University, Long Beach.

HEYDAY

from **NATIVE CALIFORNIA**

Heyday's Berkeley Roundhouse program celebrates California's diverse Indian cultures through our quarterly magazine, *News from Native California*, and books on Native life.

Since its origins, Heyday has kept California Indian peoples at the center of its work, beginning with the publication of *The Ohlone Way* by founder Malcolm Margolin in 1978 and the debut of the serial magazine *News from Native California* in 1987. In 2012 the Roundhouse program was developed within Heyday as a place to celebrate Indigenous storytelling and culture-keeping. It's heartfelt, emotional, intelligent work, significant to California tribal nations and friends.

Heyday's California Indian publishing program brings books by and about Native Californians to press. Award-winning and critically acclaimed, publications under the Roundhouse umbrella amplify the traditions, artwork, and insights of the West Coast's first peoples. From tribal memoirs to children's stories to cookbooks, these books preserve cherished knowledge and offer eye-opening perspective with integrity and deep respect.

A quarterly magazine connecting readers to the West Coast's original voices, *News from Native California* publishes essays, news stories, poems, artwork, and tribal histories about and by Indigenous people. Informing and inspiring readers since 1987, this first-of-its-kind publication celebrates and honors the culture, heritage, and social justice work of Native Californians—past, present, and future.

Contributions from friends of Heyday and community organizations make the Roundhouse program possible. Tax-deductible gifts support specific projects and provide funding to support operating expenses for both Roundhouse books and the *News from Native California* quarterly.

heydaybooks.com/roundhouse

newsfrom**native**california.com